P9-DEY-351

A Year in the Life of a DUCHESS

To Debbie Clayden

With Love

THIS IS A CARLTON BOOK

Published in 2012 by Carlton Books Limited
20 Mortimer Street
London W1T 3JW

10 9 8 7 6 5 4 3 2

Text © Carlton Books Ltd 2012
Design © Carlton Books Ltd 2012

All rights reserved. This book is sold subject to the condition that it may not be reproduced, stored in a retrieval system or transmitted in any form or by any means, electronic, mechanical, photocopying, recording or otherwise without the publisher's prior consent.

A CIP catalogue record for this book is available from the British Library.

ISBN 978 1 78097 067 7

Printed in Dubai

A Year in the Life of a DUCHESS

Catherine, HRH The Duchess of Cambridge

IAN LLOYD

CARLTON
BOOKS

Contents

Her Royal Highness The Duchess of Cambridge is presented with flowers during a trip to a UNICEF Emergency Supply Centre in November 2011 in Copenhagen.

INTRODUCTION

On 29 April 2011 Britain was gripped by wedding fever as the long awaited wedding of 29-year-old Catherine Middleton to the future King William V took place in Westminster Abbey in front of 2,000 guests and a worldwide audience of two billion viewers. *A Year in the Life of a Duchess* shows what happened after this momentous day.

Featuring over 100 images of William and Catherine's public and private engagements, this beautiful book is a celebration of Catherine's first 12 months as Her Royal Highness The Duchess of Cambridge, including the couple's first official tour to Canada and the US. The new Duchess of Cambridge was an instant success, constantly smiling, charming her hosts, shaking hands with the crowds and wearing a never-ending supply of outfits that were either designed by Canadians or depicted the country's symbols.

Back in the UK it was announced that the couple would be keeping a low profile in the run up to the Queen's Diamond Jubilee and appearances were at first limited to just one or two a month. The scarcity value only seemed to add to the fascination. Whatever Kate wore was analyzed and commented on. Some of her clothes were inevitably designer wear, but some were high street couture and often old stock whose provenance proved infuriatingly difficult for the fashion pundits to identify. Those items that were shop bought and named sold out within hours, proving that the new Duchess, like her mother-in-law before her, was rapidly becoming the UK fashion industry's greatest asset.

This last year also saw Catherine grow into her new role as a key member of the Royal Family. While William was deployed to the Falkland Islands in the spring of 2012, back home in the UK, his wife revealed more than once that she was missing him. Nevertheless her working life took on a new aspect. She accompanied the Queen on two engagements, learning the ropes from the most experienced royal lady in the world. She also carried out a succession of solo engagements as well as making her first public speech in March 2012. Once again her every appearance was without fault and drew only favourable comments.

A Year in the Life of a Duchess also reveals Catherine's private life. Home for the young couple is the picturesque island of Anglesey where the prince has managed to resume his career as a Search and Rescue pilot while Catherine is very much a military wife, running her home with the help of a part-time cleaner rather than the usual battalion of royal servants. Their life in North Wales is about as ordinary as a royal couple could ever hope to achieve. At the same time, Catherine has also worked hard to maintain close relationships with her own family and friends.

William returned to the UK in late March, and the couple enjoyed a skiing break together before coming home to prepare to celebrate the Queen's Diamond Jubilee and to support London's hosting of the Olympic Games. There was of course time for a low key celebration of their first wedding anniversary and to give thanks for a year that saw their launch onto the world's stage where they gave a confident, flawless and critically acclaimed performance.

A Royal Timeline

29 April 2011
Prince William and Miss Catherine Middleton are married in Westminster Abbey. After the cermony, they watch a flypast by the RAF over Buckingham Palace and attend a reception hosted by the Queen and later a dinner hosted by the Prince of Wales.

30 April 2011
The newlyweds leave by helicopter for a short private break.

5 May 2011
Catherine is spotted shopping in Waitrose on Anglesey.

Mid-May 2011
The couple honeymoon in the Seychelles.

24 May 2011
William and Catherine meet US President Barack Obama and his wife Michelle at a private reception at Buckingham Palace.

4 June 2011
The couple attend the Epsom Derby to see the Queen's horse run.

9 June 2011
William and Catherine attend a charity gala dinner at Kensington Palace for the charity Absolute Return for Kids (ARK).

11 June 2011
Catherine attends Trooping the Colour by carriage, William as part of the Queen's escort. Later, Catherine and her sister Pippa attend the wedding of Sam Waley-Cohen and Annabel Ballin in Berkshire.

12 June 2011
The couple attend a service in St George's Chapel, Windsor Castle, for Prince Philip's ninetieth birthday, and a reception in the castle.

13 June 2011
They attend the Order of the Garter service in St George's Chapel.

16 June 2011
Carole and Michael Middleton are guests of the Queen at Ascot.

25 June 2011
The Duke and Duchess watch a medal parade for the Irish Guards.

27 June 2011
William and Catherine attend Wimbledon to watch Britain's Andy Murray play Frenchman Richard Gasquet.

30 June 2011
The Duke and Duchess depart for a tour of Canada and the US. On arrival in Canada, they lay a wreath at the National War Memorial, Ottawa, and are guests at a dinner given by the Governor-General.

1 July 2011
The royal couple watch a citizenship ceremony at the Canadian Museum of Civilisation, Gatineau, Quebec. In the afternoon they enjoy the Canada Day celebration in Ottawa.

2 July 2011
They attend a reception for war veterans at the Canadian War Museum, Ottawa, and visit Sainte-Justine University Hospital, Montreal, and l'Institut de Tourisme et d'Hotellerie du Quebec.

3 July 2011
The Duke and Duchess attend a service on HMS *Montreal* on the St Lawrence, Quebec City, and visit la Maison Dauphine youth centre.

4 July 2011
The couple visit Prince Edward Island. William joins a helicopter exercise with the Canadian Air Force at Dalvay-by-the-Sea.

5 July 2011
The Duke and Duchess visit Yellowknife in the Northwest Territories, where they meet Canadian Rangers and students studying the Dechinta Programme at Blachford Lake.

7 July 2011
The royal couple stop in Alberta where they visit the ward of the 21st Century Research and Innovation Centre at Calgary before attending a dinner given by Prime Minister Stephen Harper.

8 July 2011
William and Catherine attend the Calgary Stampede and a reception with the Premier of Alberta, then lay a wreath at Challenger Rotary Park, Calgary. Flying on to Los Angeles, they attend a reception in support of UK Trade and Investment.

9 July 2011
The couple watch a charity Polo Match in Santa Barbara, then attend a dinner at LA's Belasco Theater.

10 July 2011
William and Catherine lunch in Beverly Hills with patrons of the Tusk Trust, and visit Inner-City Arts in LA. Their final visit is to Service Nation: Mission Serve recruitment fair at Sony Pictures.

22 July 2011
Catherine's wedding dress is displayed at Buckingham Palace.

29/30 July 2011
William and Catherine are guests at Zara Phillips and Mike Tindall's pre-wedding reception on the royal yacht *Britannia*, at Leith in Edinburgh, and at the wedding itself the next day.

19 August 2011
The couple meet local people affected by the summer riots in Winson Green, Birmingham, and in Birmingham city centre.

25 September 2011
William and Catherine attend the wedding of their friends Thomas Sutton and Harriet Colthurst in Wilton, Wiltshire.

29 September 2011
The couple open the Oak Centre for Children and Young People at the Royal Marsden Hospital, Sutton, Surrey.

13 October 2011
The Duke (patron) and Duchess attend a dinner for "100 Women in Hedge Funds" Philanthropic Initiatives at St James's Palace.

26 October 2011
Catherine carries out her first solo engagement, hosting a dinner at Clarence House for the charity In Kind Direct.

2 November 2011
The Duke and Duchess visit Denmark. After lunch with the Crown Prince and Princess, they visit a UNICEF distribution centre for East Africa famine relief.

10 November 2011
William (patron of the National Memorial Arboretum Future Foundations Appeal) and Catherine attend an appeal dinner.

13 November 2011
Remembrance Day: the couple pay respects at the Cenotaph.

28 November 2011
The couple take part in a reception for the media to mark the 2012 Diamond Jubilee.

6 December 2011
They enjoy a concert at the Royal Albert Hall in aid of the Prince's Trust and the Foundation of Prince William and Prince Harry.

19 December 2011
The couple are guests at a Christmas lunch at Buckingham Palace for all the royal family. They later attend *The Sun* Military Awards Ceremony at the Imperial War Museum in London.

21 December 2011
The Duke and Duchess visit Centrepoint Camberwell Foyer.

25 December 2011
William and Catherine join senior royals at church at Sandringham.

31 December 2011
William and Catherine spend New Year with the Middletons.

8 January 2012
The couple attend the premiere of the film *War Horse* in London.

Mid-January
They holiday in Mustique.

2 February 2012
William arrives in the Falkland Islands for a six-week deployment. Catherine makes a private visit to Clouds House near Salisbury, a treatment centre run by Action on Addiction in Wiltshire.

8 February 2012
The Duchess visits the National Portrait Gallery's Lucian Freud Portraits exhibition in London.

14 February 2012
Catherine visits Liverpool, taking in alcohol-free bar The Brink and Alder Hey Children's Hospital.

21 February 2012
Catherine visits Oxford-based charity The Art Room's classrooms at Rose Hill Primary School, and Oxford Spires Academy School.

1 March 2012
Catherine accompanies the Queen and the Duchess of Cornwall on a visit to Fortnum and Mason, Piccadilly, London.

8 March 2012
Catherine joins the Queen and Prince Philip on a visit to Leicester on the first day of the Queen's Diamond Jubilee tour.

17 March 2012
Catherine makes her first public speech, at a hospice in Suffolk.

THE WEDDING

An estimated two billion people watched the royal wedding on TV, mobile phones, laptops, YouTube and on every other conceivable form of modern broadcasting media. Five thousand street parties took place throughout the UK and one million people packed the processional route from Buckingham Palace to Westminster Abbey. Film crews came from as far afield as Brazil and the Ukraine and photographers paid up to £1,000 for the prime spot opposite the palace balcony to capture that much-anticipated kiss.

LEFT: *The future King William V and Queen Catherine pose with their families in the Throne Room at Buckingham Palace for a formal wedding photograph. Front row (L-R): Grace van Cutsem, Eliza Lopes (Camilla's granddaughter), Prince Philip Duke of Edinburgh, Queen Elizabeth II, Margarita Armstrong-Jones (the Queen's great niece), Lady Louise Windsor (daughter of Prince Edward) and William Lowther-Pinkerton. Back Row (L-R): Tom Pettifer, Camilla Duchess of Cornwall, Prince Charles, Prince Harry, Michael Middleton, Carole Middleton, James Middleton and Philippa Middleton.*

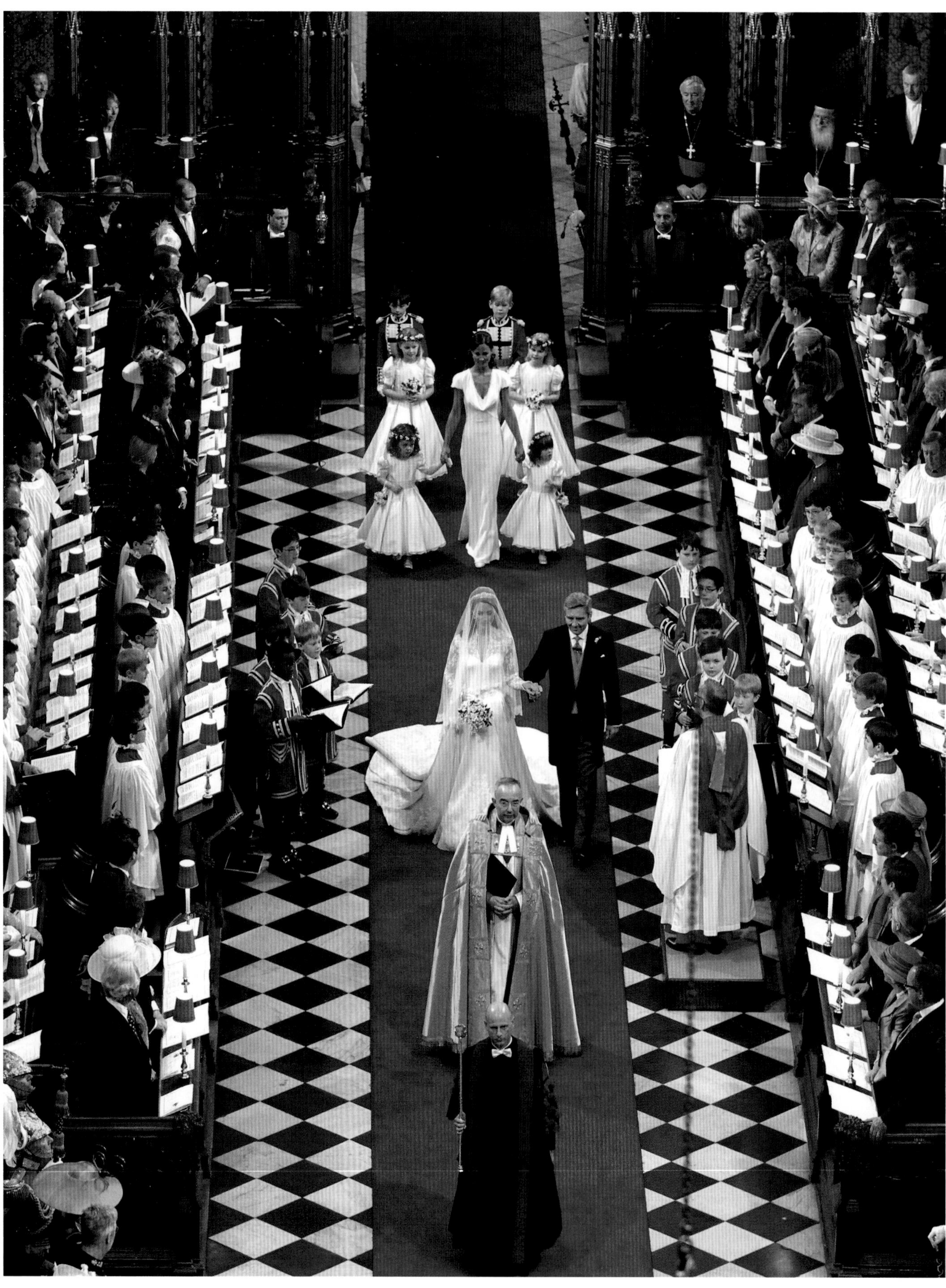

LEFT: *The newlyweds prepare to leave the Abbey watched by the entire British Royal Family and European royals including Queen Margretha of Denmark (top right wearing kingfisher blue). The bride had arrived as plain Catherine Middleton and was now preparing to face the future as Her Royal Highness the Duchess of Cambridge.*

Why was the wedding of William Arthur Philip Louis Windsor to Catherine Elizabeth Middleton such a global phenomenon? The most obvious answer is that it had it all. It had the magnetic combination of royalty, style, glamour, pageantry and, perhaps most important of all, it was clearly a love match.

William's parents only dated each other for a year or so before 20-year-old Lady Diana Spencer made that terrifying walk down the nave of St Paul's Cathedral, "like a lamb to slaughter", as she told biographer Andrew Morton. Prince Andrew and Sarah Ferguson were also romantically linked for just a year before their Abbey wedding in 1986, as had Princess Anne and Mark Phillips been a decade earlier. All three marriages ended in 1992 – the year described by the Queen as an "annus horribilis" – when Anne was divorced and it was announced that Andrew and "Fergie" and then Charles and Diana were to separate.

BELOW: *Catherine looking relaxed and composed as she mingles with guests at a lunchtime reception hosted by the Queen at Buckingham Palace following the wedding. Here she chats to the Governor-General of Canada, His Excellency the Rt Hon David Johnston and Mrs Sharon Johnston, and no doubt the royal couple's forthcoming Canadian tour was a subject of conversation.*

ABOVE: *In a surprise break with tradition, William borrowed his father's beloved open-topped Aston Martin for the short drive from Buckingham Palace to Clarence House. By now William had changed into a Blues and Royals captain's frock coat, but Catherine delighted the crowds by remaining in her wedding dress.*

By the time William and Catherine met at the very beginning of the twenty-first century, the House of Windsor was beginning to change. Precedent and protocol were ignored and royal couples were allowed to get to know each other well and were not steamrollered into marriage. It began when Prince Edward met public relations worker Sophie Rhys-Jones in 1993. Edward and Sophie were a couple for a full six years before they married in June 1999. The last royal bride of the twentieth century had been fully schooled in all aspects of life with the Windsors at the same time as she was slowly getting to know her husband-to-be in the way any other woman would.

William and Catherine's romance was even more slow-burning than his uncle and aunt's. They split up twice, first as students at St Andrews University and then again in the spring of 2007 when William felt trapped. Free to go his own way, the prince discovered that life on the nightclub circuit, while undoubtedly fun, was not the way he was going to meet a future wife with the qualities of a queen consort.

Back together again by August of the same year, the couple re-established a low-key romantic life away from the fast lane and the ever-present paparazzi. Life for them then, and now, is a world away from that led by Charles and Diana. Instead, they are as near to an ordinary couple as their position allows –

content to eat a pizza in front of the TV in their Anglesey hideaway rather than join the A-list circuit in London.

This combination of the ordinary and the extraordinary seems to fascinate people. We know they are clearly the best of friends, university mates who have clicked, like so many of their St Andrews contemporaries did. Yet we also know that one day they will succeed to the British throne – and whatever Commonwealth realms still survive – as King William V and Queen Catherine.

It was this mixture of the ordinary and extraordinary – the private and the public – that was so evident at the royal wedding. There were the traditional hymns, the Archbishop of Canterbury conducting the ceremony, the curtsey to the Queen, the RAF flypast and the 1902 State Landau – the same carriage used by William's parents – for the return journey.

But there was also the new, the innovative and the very personal side to this wedding. The couple prepared their own prayer in which they thanked God "for our families, for the love that we share and for the joy of our marriage". They also asked the Almighty to "keep our eyes fixed on what is real and important in life" and to "help us to serve and comfort those who suffer".

BELOW: *Prince Harry had decorated his father's car with balloons, ribbons and this distinctive number plate.*

LEFT: *On the evening of the wedding, Catherine prepares to leave Clarence House for a private dinner party for 300 close friends and family. The new Duchess of Cambridge had changed into a flowing white satin gown, accessorized with a diamante detail at the waist and an angora bolero cardigan. Like her wedding dress, it was also designed by Sarah Burton of Alexander McQueen.*

ABOVE: *After spending their first night as man and wife at Buckingham Palace, the next morning the couple walk hand-in-hand to a waiting helicopter as they leave for a secret honeymoon location.*

The innovative side was most obvious in aspects of the décor of the ceremony. Under other circumstances Catherine Middleton would have married near her family home at Bucklebury in Berkshire. Bucklebury Common is famous for its Avenue of Oaks at Chapel Row and in Westminster Abbey eight 6-metre- (20-foot-) high trees – six maple and two hornbeam – replicated that avenue, bringing rural England into the heart of London.

The wedding reception was similarly more personal than the "wedding breakfast" that palace staff traditionally create for the royal party and their closest friends. For the weddings of the Queen and Queen Mother, for instance, only a small fraction of the guests could attend the sit-down meal. William and Kate opted for a more relaxed, buffet-style reception hosted by the Queen for around 650 guests.

That's not to say the reception wasn't lavish. Mark Flanagan, the royal chef, aided by a team of 21 other chefs, prepared 10,000 mouthwatering canapés. Guests were served, among other things, Pressed Duck Terrine with Fruit Chutney, Smoked Scottish Salmon Rose on Beetroot Blini, Langoustines with Lemon Mayonnaise, Pressed Confit of Pork Belly and Bubble and Squeak with Confit Shoulder of Lamb. This feast was washed down with

Pol Roger NV Brut Réserve Champagne as well as a selection of other soft and alcoholic drinks.

Instead of being trapped at a top table in the palace ballroom, William and Catherine were free to wander through the State Apartments to talk to friends and relatives, while in the background Claire Jones, the official harpist to the Prince of Wales, provided the subtle ambient music.

The couple cut the official wedding cake designed by Fiona Cairns. Made from 17 individual fruit cakes, 12 of which formed the base, it had eight tiers and was decorated in cream and white icing. Fiona added 900 individual flowers including the English rose, Scottish thistle, Welsh daffodil and Irish shamrock. Again, with that mixture of formal and informal that characterized this wedding, the couple also cut a chocolate biscuit cake – William's favourite – created for the prince by McVitie's from a royal family recipe.

After the reception ended at 3.35pm, William drove his new bride the short distance from Buckingham Palace to Clarence House. In another personal touch, Prince Charles had allowed his son to drive his beloved two-seater Aston Martin BD6 which was decorated with balloons by Prince Harry and given the

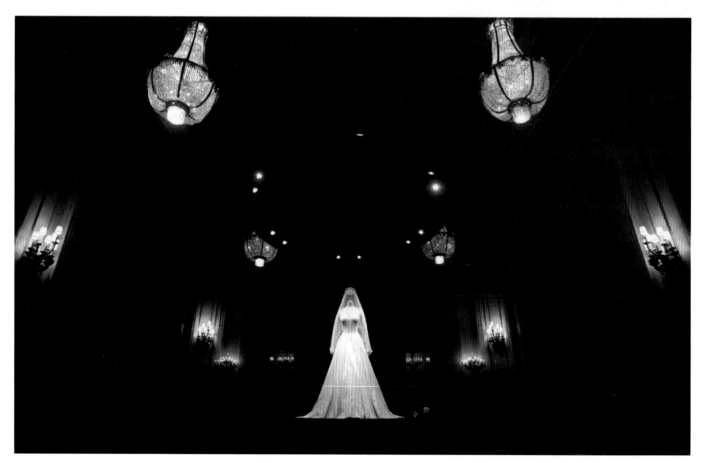

rear number plate "JU5T WED" for the day. A few months later it emerged that William caused his father to wince by roaring off with the handbrake still on.

The groom had changed into the frock coat of a Blues and Royals captain but Kate still wore her wedding dress, to the delight of the crowd who had a second chance to see it. Overhead a yellow Sea King helicopter flying the RAF ensign dipped in salute to the couple – a surprise organized by RAF Wattisham to honour the UK's most famous search and rescue pilot.

Later the couple returned to Buckingham Palace to attend an evening reception hosted by Prince Charles. The Queen had by now left to allow the younger generation to relax at a less formal party for close friends and the younger royals.

Kate wore an evening dress designed by Sarah Burton who had also created her wedding dress. It was a strapless white dress with a fitted bodice and an embroidered waistband. Over her shoulders she wore an elegant shrug to keep off the slight chill of a late spring evening. After dinner the couple partied until the small hours. Singer-songwriter Ellie Goulding performed at the event and her cover version of the Elton John classic "Your Song" was William and Kate's first dance. The evening ended at 3am with a small fireworks display in the palace grounds.

Having spent their first night as man and wife in Buckingham Palace, the following morning the couple left by helicopter for what was described by a spokesperson for Prince William as "a private destination". In contrast to the day before, when a million onlookers cheered them on the way to the Abbey, only two footmen were on hand to say goodbye to William and Kate as they emerged hand-in-hand from the palace and strolled to the helicopter in bright sunshine. For this most private of public couples it was just the sort of restrained departure they had wanted.

Later in the year Kate's wedding dress was again centre stage when it was announced it would be the star attraction of the annual summer opening of the Buckingham Palace State Apartments. Before the exhibition was opened to the public there was a private viewing for two VIP guests, Queen Elizabeth II and the bride herself, the future Queen Catherine.

Something about the ghost-like appearance of the headless mannequin used to exhibit the gown seemed to upset the Queen, who was overheard by film crew to describe it as "horrible" adding, "It's made to look very creepy". Kate bravely chipped in with her own opinion, saying it had a "3D effect". For once the public disagreed with the monarch. By the end of the day on which it was announced that the wedding dress was to be exhibited, a spokesman for the Royal Collection said, "It's incredible, the phones have been in melt-down for advance tickets."

Wedding fever proved hard to shake off and a new expression – "the Kate effect" – was linked to everything from British fashion to the sale of souvenirs.

TOP LEFT: *Tourists queue outside Buckingham Palace as it opens to the public for the summer exhibition on 23 July 2011, at which the star attraction was the royal wedding dress.*

LEFT: *The famous dress complete with its veil and tiara and 2.7-metre (nine-foot) train was displayed on a raised oval stage.*

ABOVE: *The Queen and Catherine paid a private visit to see the dress and other wedding memorabilia on 22 July, the day before the exhibition opened to the public. It appeared the mannequin's lack of a head may have perturbed the Queen.*

BACK TO WORK

The new Duchess of Cambridge went from being the "bride of the century" to being a housewife in fewer than three days.

LEFT: *Catherine launches the new Hereford Endeavour lifeboat as well as her royal career. A lifetime of plantings, openings, namings and, of course, launches lie ahead but the future queen doesn't look daunted despite the strong breeze.*

While bets were placed on where exactly the "private destination" was as they left Buckingham Palace by helicopter, all the prince's office would say was that it wasn't an overseas holiday. A St James's Palace spokesman said: "The Duke and Duchess of Cambridge have chosen not to depart for a honeymoon immediately. Instead, after spending the weekend privately in the United Kingdom, the Duke will return to work as a search and rescue pilot next week.".

The honeymoon delay was in part so William could show his commitment to his search and rescue programme but also to avoid the momentum that followed his parents' wedding, when the media tried desperately to track down the couple at every stop on their Royal Yacht *Britannia* cruise.

Home for William and Catherine is a modest whitewashed cottage near William's base at RAF Valley on the island of Anglesey, which they rent for £750 a month. The prince returned to work on the Tuesday after the wedding. One of his colleagues, Sergeant Ed Griffiths, said: "He'll be coming back down to earth. We'll be going out on rescues and getting on with things as usual." Within 48 hours William was involved in two dramatic air rescues. He was part of an RAF Sea King helicopter crew which rescued a 70-year-old man who had

BELOW: *A typically isolated and rugged beach near RAF Valley in Anglesey where William is based. The royal couple have grown to love this peaceful idyll that offers spectacular views and where the respectful locals leave them in peace.*

ABOVE: *Prince William takes the controls of a Sea King helicopter on 14 April 2011 in Holyhead, Wales. The prince is committed to his career as a Search and Rescue Pilot until at least 2013. Last November he was involved in a frantic rescue mission to save Russian crewmen after a cargo ship sank in the Irish Sea.*

suffered a heart attack while climbing 890-metre- (2,946-foot-) high Lliwedd in Snowdonia. Having airlifted him to hospital, the team returned to help four policemen off Snowdonia. The men, all walkers in their twenties, were on the narrow Crib Goch ridge when one of them developed severe vertigo.

Catherine, meanwhile, was spotted shopping in her local Waitrose store just six days after the royal wedding, prompting the witty tabloid headline "Kate Heads Down the Aisle Again". She may be a duchess and Her Royal Highness, with a brand new biography on the Palace website, but on the Thursday after her return to Anglesey she was snapped "trolley surfing" in the supermarket car park like any other customer.

Dressed in French Sole mock croc ballet pumps, black Hudson skinny jeans and a sage-green frilled shrug over her white cashmere jumper, she spent half an hour in the Menai Bridge supermarket, buying a healthy selection of fruit and veg. While locals gave her a few double takes, Kate happily got on with the job in hand. The only clue to her royal status was the flash of colour from Princess Diana's sapphire engagement ring and, of course, the three police bodyguards trying to mingle unobtrusively with the morning shoppers.

Besides supermarket shopping at Waitrose, Tesco and Morrisons, Kate has also sourced local produce. According to one butcher on the island, she likes to bake William meat pies complete with gravy made from scratch. "She is a good

shopper", newspapers quoted the butcher as saying, "she knows what she is doing. She was in here after the wedding and she bought some meat and 82p of lamb's liver to make the pie gravy. I said: 'Are you sure you can afford that?' And she said: 'I can now'."

Not everything is homemade. She and William were once caught on security cameras buying pizza and frozen chips at the 24-hour branch of Spar at the Valley crossroads, the nearest large shop to where they live. Kate is happy to play the part of an officer's wife and begin married life in a low-key fashion. She has no housekeeper, maid or chauffeur, although she does have a part-time cleaner. Everything else she is content to do herself.

"She has always been happy to support William," a royal source said at the time of the wedding, adding: "that is one of the reasons they make such a good couple. She enjoys cooking and has a really good eye for decorating so has enjoyed making their cottage homely.

"One thing they're very keen on is they can go back to having a private life in between public engagements and, with its remote beaches and countryside, Anglesey is perfect for that. They just like to do normal things, go walking, go shopping and have a drink at their local pubs."

Comparisons have been made with the Queen who, on and off for two years between 1949 and 1951, spent an idyllic time as an officer's wife on another island – Malta. Prince Philip was stationed there while he was still in

ABOVE: *The look of love. William and Catherine attend the naming ceremony and of the Atlantic 85 Hereford Endeavour at Trearddur Bay Lifeboat Station, Anglesey on 24 February 2011. It was fitting that one of their first public appearances following their engagement should be on the island they call home.*

RIGHT: *The present Queen as Princess Elizabeth enjoyed her own island paradise in the early days of her marriage. Her husband Prince Philip, Duke of Edinburgh was stationed with the Royal Navy at Malta and the princess paid several lengthy visits between 1949 and 1951.*

full-time service with the Royal Navy and Princess Elizabeth stayed at Villa Guardamangia, the home of Philip's uncle, Earl Mountbatten of Burma. Elizabeth enjoyed the novelty of having her hair done in the local salon and walking into town for a meal in a restaurant or to see a movie.

William and Kate's life is not entirely dissimilar to that enjoyed by his grandparents. They are occasionally spotted at local bars and restaurants. Before their marriage they would call at the White Eagle gastropub in Rhoscolyn where William enjoyed a burger and a local beer while Kate sipped wine with her fish or salad.

There are also occasional trips to the cinema. They travelled to Llandudno on the mainland to watch the summer box-office hit *Bridesmaids* at Cineworld. The cinema later confirmed the visit on its Twitter account: "Prince William & Kate Middy saw Bridesmaids at Cineworld Llandudno this W'end. Wonder what they made of Kristen Wiigs 'one eyed' impression?" The couple have also watched

ABOVE: *The White Eagle pub at Rhoscolyn, Anglesey, where William and Catherine have been spotted enjoying a romantic dinner, though they are just as happy with a pizza and a glass of wine at home.*

Harry Potter and the Deathly Hallows: Part 2 and in August were spotted laughing uncontrollably as they joined a packed house to see *The Inbetweeners.*

William and Kate are a tremendous advert for Anglesey and North Wales in general. Despite the fact that the majority of tourists aren't able even to snatch a fleeting glimpse of the couple, interest in their island paradise has prompted a wave of attention. Esther Roberts of North Wales Tourism says: "In the aftermath of the wedding, overseas tourist enquiries at the Anglesey Tourist Information centre went up by 18 per cent. Online enquiries doubled over the year, but in the April to June period were up by 400 per cent. The local people respect and guard William and Kate's privacy and tourists would never be given any information by residents".

No one should underestimate the effect having the world's most glamorous

BELOW: *William's parents spent their honeymoon on board the Royal Yacht* Britannia. *Here they about to embark on their Mediterranean cruise, having flown from Southampton on 1 August 1981 to join the yacht at Gibraltar.*

ABOVE: *The Republic of Seychelles, an archipelago nation of over 115 islands located in the Indian Ocean. This was where William and Catherine enjoyed an idyllic, romantic honeymoon undisturbed by the press or other tourists.*

couple calling Anglesey "home" has done for the island. Says Esther: "They have increased the profile of Anglesey as a holiday destination and given the island enormous media coverage, particularly at the time of the wedding. Undoubtedly the long-term value will outweigh even the immediate benefits."

According to Pip Cockeram, a consultant to the Anglesey Tourism Association, "a clue to the couple's value to tourism can be seen in holiday statistics for the island. Since April, bookings for hotels, guesthouses and caravan sites have soared to almost 40 per cent over the 2010 figure. This works out at nearly £90 million in extra income from visitors to Anglesey alone."

The couple finally left for their honeymoon nearly two weeks after their wedding, flying to their island paradise in the Seychelles. Bets had been placed on William and Catherine flying to one of their "usual" resorts, including Mustique, the Caribbean island much loved by Princess Margaret, or Kenya where William proposed to Kate. When news of the destination broke, bookmakers Ladbrokes paid out £1,000 to a customer who put £30 on the less likely Seychelles at odds of 33/1.

The Seychelles did have special significance for William and Kate, however, since it was here, in 2007, that they enjoyed a make-or-break holiday following their temporary split. For that holiday they spent a week on the idyllic island of Desroches, 240 kilometres (150 miles) by helicopter from the main island of Mahé. This time the Cambridges slipped quietly away from their Anglesey home on Monday 9 May before catching a plane for the Indian Ocean archipelago, and then transferring by helicopter, again from Mahé.

Although Clarence House confirmed that the couple had left for honeymoon and that Prince William was due two weeks' leave from duty in accordance with RAF policy, William's office refused to say where they were heading. Unfortunately, they hadn't banked on the Seychelles' Ministry of Tourism, which issued a statement to the media via its spokeswoman:

"We are obviously delighted that Prince William and his new wife have decided to honeymoon in the Seychelles. We know they will want some peace and quiet and there couldn't be a better place for them to find it. We will leave them to enjoy themselves throughout their stay. Perhaps at some stage our tourism chief executive might meet with them but otherwise we have nothing special planned for their holiday."

Royal officials would only confirm the honeymoon destination after the couple had safely returned to the UK. "The Duke and Duchess of Cambridge thoroughly enjoyed their time together," said William's spokesman, "and are grateful to the Seychelles government for their assistance in making the honeymoon such a memorable and special ten days." They were particularly grateful to the Seychelles coastguard who helped ensure William and Kate were undisturbed during their stay and on the final day the couple invited the coastguard ashore to meet them and to personally thank them for their help. They then flew back to the UK and on to their other island paradise – the one they call home.

CANADA

It was back in early February 2011, ten weeks before the royal wedding and with only one joint public engagement under their belt, that it was announced that William and Catherine would visit Canada in June. If the decision to launch the Duchess onto the world's stage so soon after the wedding was a surprise, the choice of Canada was far less surprising.

LEFT: *William and Catherine join in Canada Day celebrations at Parliament Hill, Ottawa, on 1 July 2011. The Duchess's choice of a hat and coat to match the Canadian flag shows she's already mastered the art of fashion diplomacy.*

In 1951 another glamorous couple, the then Princess Elizabeth and Prince Philip, made their first overseas tour to Canada with a similar two-day stopover in the United States. The shy princess found it more arduous than she'd expected. The local press, used to her mother's charm and easy smile, complained that she was too serious, and her Private Secretary, Martin Charteris, tried to encourage her to smile. An exasperated Elizabeth said: "My face is aching with smiling." To try and ease the tension, the Duke of Edinburgh chased his wife through the corridors of the Canadian royal train wearing a set of false teeth.

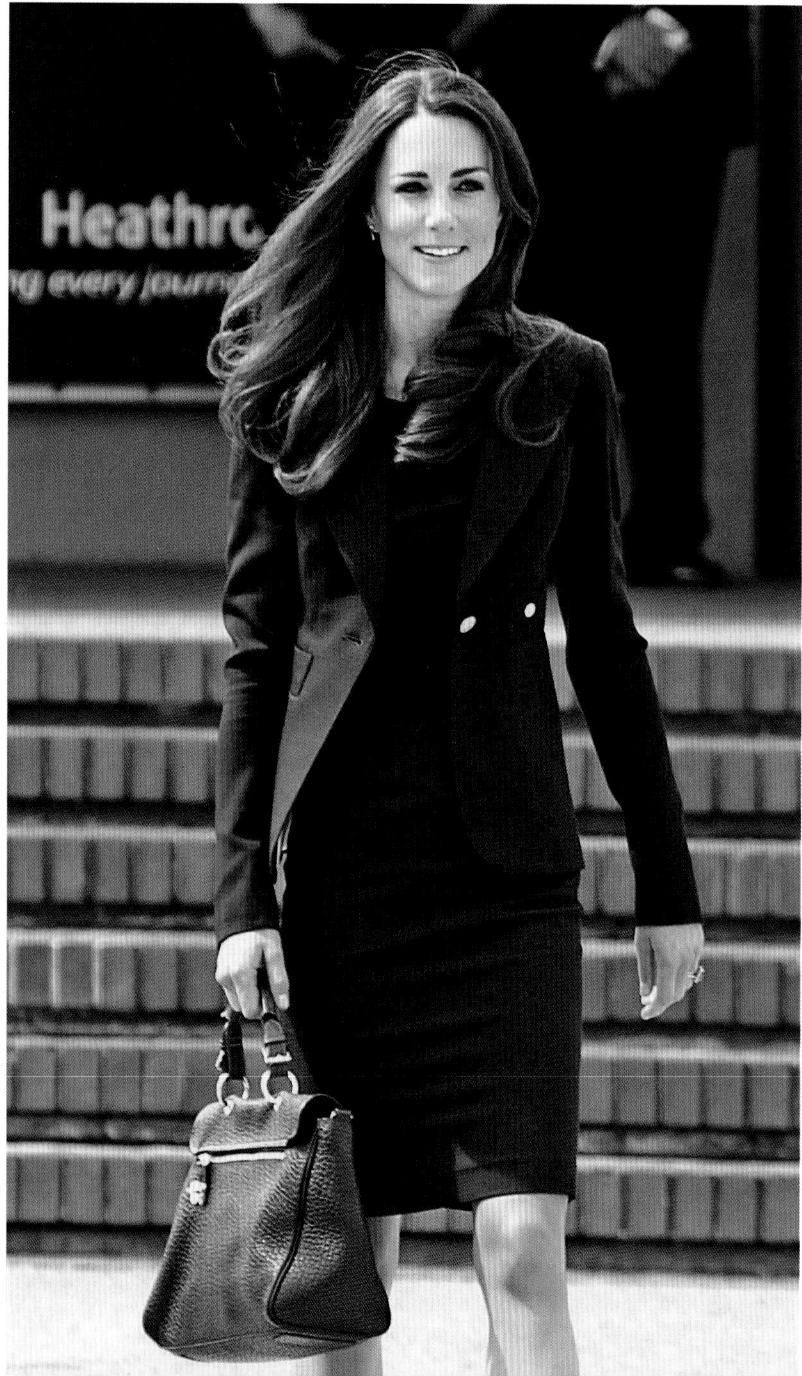

LEFT: *Looking ready for business, Catherine arrives at London's Heathrow Airport on 30 June 2011 to board a plane of the Royal Canadian Air Force for her first royal overseas tour.*

RIGHT: *William and Catherine arrive at Rideau Hall in Ottawa, Ontario with David Johnston (standing on the right), Governor General of Canada, at the start of their nine-day tour of Canada.*

ABOVE: *A red carpet welcome for the royal couple as they arrive on Parliament Hill, Ottawa to attend Canada Day celebrations on the second day of the tour.*

Three decades later Prince Andrew, Duke of York, was accompanied on a tour of Canada by his new wife Sarah on her first overseas trip. In those days "Fergie" was very popular and her down-to-earth humour and zest for life were seen as assets. Again, there were strains along the way. Sarah recounted in her autobiography, *My Story*, the sheer tedium of always having to look good in public. She wrote that her "dress requirements alone would have sent a saner woman screaming to the nearest exit", adding that "after ten days of ceaseless changing I was ready to burn the lot of them".

Certainly no one in February could have predicted how well Kate would cope with the rigours of the tour or how William would feel if everyone wanted to meet his wife and he was sidelined – as Charles had soon realized was a fact of life on his tours with Diana.

Prince William has great memories of his childhood visits to Canada. In 1991, nine-year-old William and seven-year-old Harry flew out to join their parents on a five-day tour of Ontario. The photos of Diana, arms outstretched, running to greet her boys on the deck of the Royal Yacht *Britannia* were among the defining images of the Waleses' marriage in its final stages.

The prince returned in 1998, when he was 16, in the aftermath of Diana's death. He was a reluctant teen heart-throb, peering shyly from under his fringe in a way so reminiscent of his mother. There was a brief official welcome with a jokey exchange of baseball caps between William, Harry and Charles, and then all three princes were allowed a peaceful holiday, away from the cameras, on the ski slopes of Whistler in British Columbia.

William and Kate began their historic tour on 30 June when their Canadian Air Force jet landed at Ottawa airport and the couple were greeted by Stephen Harper, the Canadian Prime Minister.

Already the media was abuzz with the news that Kate had boarded the plane wearing a navy blue dress called the "Manon" by the French designer Roland Mouret, teamed with a navy blazer by the Canadian fashion house Smythe Les Vestes. This was serious sartorial flattery and there was more to follow when they

BELOW: *Smiles all round as the Duke and Duchess attend a citizenship ceremony at Ottawa's Museum of Civilisation.*

landed since, for her all-important arrival, Kate had changed into a navy lace dress made by Montreal-born Erdem Moralioglu.

The couple's first act – even before their official welcome – was to lay a wreath at the Tomb of the Unknown Soldier at the National War Memorial. The following day was Canada Day and Catherine, who was not scheduled to make any speeches during the tour, instead let her fashion do the talking. She wore a white Reiss dress and a red maple-leaf hat to the delight of the 300,000-strong crowd and the fashion pundits. She also wore the diamond maple-leaf brooch that had been presented to the Queen Mother on her first Canadian tour in 1939. It is now a favourite of the Queen, who loaned it to Catherine for the visit.

BELOW: *Day three of the tour and William takes the hands-on approach during a cooking workshop at the* Institut De Tourisme et D'hotellerie Du Quebec *in Montreal while, at the top of the table, Catherine awaits instructions.*

William spoke for both himself and Catherine at Rideau Hall, where they were to stay for the first part of their tour, when he said: "We are so looking forward to this adventure." He then spoke in French, Canada's second official language. What William lacked in linguistic skill he made up for in enthusiasm, at one point breaking off to say in English: "Don't worry, it'll improve…"

The start of his second speech was more rock star than royalty: "Bonjour Ottawa! Bonjour Canada! Bonne fête Canada!" It was also an opportunity to reflect on what the country meant to both his family and to his wife's family: "I'm excited to be able to share this with Catherine," he said to wild applause, "because she has told me that she feels exactly the same way. She heard about Canada not from her parents, but from her grandfather, a wonderful man who passed away last year, but who held this country dear to his heart – for he trained in Alberta as a young pilot during the Second World War." He also passed on the Queen's "warmest good wishes to the people of Canada" and said

BELOW: *Deep in concentration, William and Catherine seem oblivious to the surrounding press and dignitaries as they visit a children's cancer ward at Sainte-Justine University Hospital in Montreal on 2 July 2011.*

ABOVE: *The future King and Queen of Canada disembark from HMCS* Montreal *in Chaplain Harbour to visit Quebec City on the fourth day of the tour.*

she "has taken a great interest in the themes and programme of our tour, and looks forward to following our progress as it unfolds".

The next stage of the tour was the province of Quebec which, as his grandmother knows from her many visits, usually guarantees protests from French separatists. There were boos from separatists when William and Catherine arrived at Sainte-Justine Hospital in Montreal, but it was estimated that loyalists outnumbered the separatists by eight to one and the riot police were more of a precaution than a necessity.

Later the couple donned chefs' uniforms and took part in a different type of demonstration when they prepared food at a cookery workshop at the Quebec Tourism and Hotel Institute. William created a herb-and-cranberry-crusted lamb confit and an impressive lobster soufflé while Catherine produced a tray of hors d'oeuvres.

It was while she was at Fort-de-Levis, meeting veterans, that the Duchess made one of those throwaway comments that is eagerly seized on by the media. When ex-pat David Cheater introduced his two-year-old daughter Raffaela to Kate, he also wished her the best in starting a family of her own. The Duchess replied: "Yes, I hope to," which naturally led to dozens of "Kate is Broody" headlines.

The couple moved on to Prince Edward Island where William flew a Sea King helicopter over Dalvay Lake for over an hour as he practised the search and rescue emergency-landing manoeuvre known as "waterbirding". A proud Kate recorded her husband's efforts with her own camera. Later in the day they both took part in a dragon boat race, competing against each other in separate boats. Although William's team won, they jointly collected the victor's bottle of champagne.

The couple moved on to Yellowknife, Northwest Territories, the land of the midnight sun, and the home of seven different aboriginal groups. William spoke the languages of Dene and Inuit and they were presented with hand-made gifts; Kate was given a pair of beaded moccasins and said diplomatically: "I will treasure them."

If there were any lingering doubts about the overall popularity of the visit, they were swept away on day seven of the tour when, instead of taking a day off as was apparently scheduled, William and Catherine made a private visit to Slave Lake in Alberta which had been ravaged by wildfire six weeks before, destroying 400 households. They had a private meeting with those who had been affected before a public walkabout among the rest of the townsfolk.

BELOW: *The couple met all age groups from Second World War veterans to infants during their tour, but there was a definite emphasis on youth. Here the couple pose with homeless and other young people at a drop-in centre in Quebec City on 3 July.*

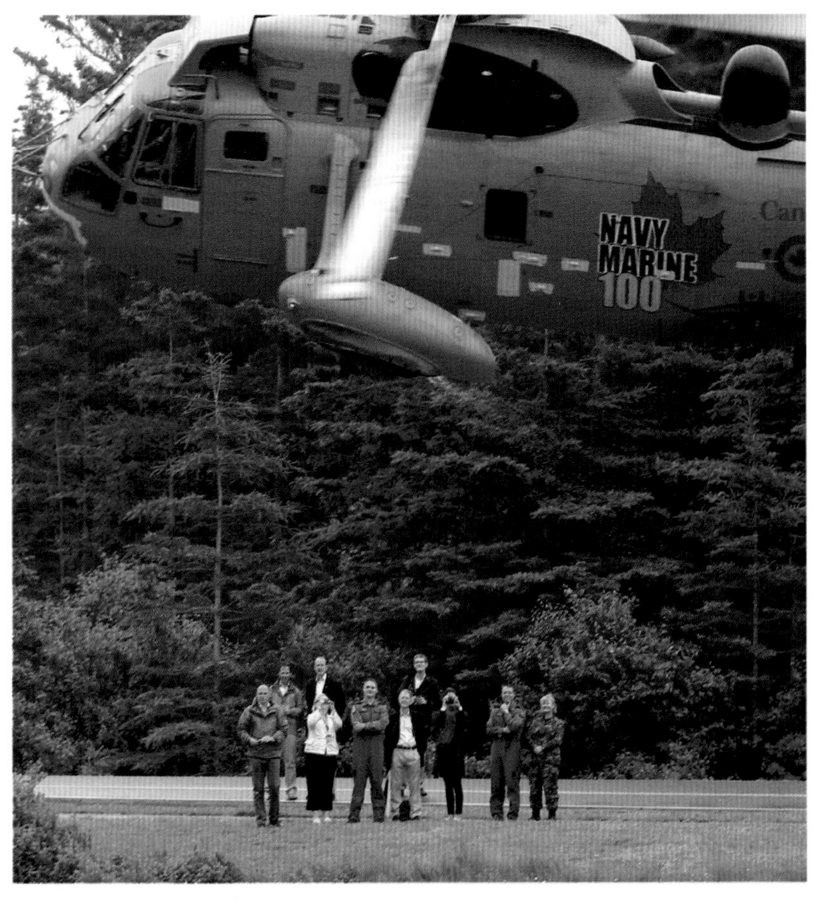

LEFT: *Home from home. William takes part in an exercise in a Sea King Helicopter at Dalvay Lake, Charlottestown on Day five of the tour. 4 July*

BELOW: *One for the family album. A proud Catherine snaps away with her camera as her husband performs a "waterbird" landing in a helicopter for the first time.*

RIGHT: *Now it's your turn! Catherine joined the prince in a dragon boat race on Dalvay Lake, Prince Edward Island. The couple rowed for separate teams and a jubilant William and co finished a third of a boat's length ahead of Catherine's team.*

MUSTANG
SURVIVAL

LEFT: *Kate used to play hockey at school and was only too happy to throw the puck for this game at Somba K'e Civic Plaza, Yellowknife on day six of the tour. William joined in with one of the games but Catherine's beige Malene Birger dress and nude LK Bennett shoes weren't too practical for the rough-and-tumble match.*

BELOW LEFT: *The couple were able to sneak away for a private break on an island on Blachford Lake, in the Northwest Territory. Here they set off by canoe for some time alone. Guiding them there was Francois Paulette (in the stern of the boat) who took them to a private lodge where they enjoyed a few hours of privacy.*

BELOW: *A tender moment as William helps Catherine adjust the red jackets they were given during their visit to a Canadian Rangers' station on Blachford Lake, on the sixth day of the tour.*

The couple did manage to escape for an overnight visit to secluded Skoki Lodge in Banff National Park to experience, if only for a short time, life in the Canadian Rockies. The day before they had also enjoyed a private three-hour sojourn on Eagle Island on Blanchford Lake, which they paddled to by canoe before enjoying a dinner of caribou steaks and whitefish, cooked on an open fire.

Like the Queen and the Yorks on their first visit to Canada, the Cambridges attended the world-famous Calgary Stampede, wearing the traditional white cowboy hats and arriving by stage coach for a reception on the evening before the stampede. The following day they set off the firework display and an explosion of ticker tape to begin the stampede.

On their final night in Canada, William made a touching speech in which he revealed they had both fallen in love with this country as much as previous generations of royals had. "In 1939, my great-grandmother, Queen Elizabeth the Queen Mother, said of her first tour of Canada with her husband King George VI, 'Canada made us'. Catherine and I now know very well what she meant. Canada has far surpassed all that we were promised. Our promise to Canada is that we shall return."

RIGHT: *The couple very much look the part in their his and hers Stetsons as they press the button to launch the Calgary Stampede on the ninth day of the tour.*

BELOW: *William and Kate were guests of the Canadian Prime Minister, Stephen Harper (in the blue shirt, standing on the right of the couple), as they watch a rodeo demonstration at the BMO Centre in Calgary. William told guests that Canada had "far surpassed all that we were promised".*

FAR RIGHT: *Kate once more wears Canada red and the Queen's diamond Maple Leaf Brooch as the couple wave farewell at Calgary airport on 8 July. In his final speech William said: "Our promise to Canada is that we shall return."*

CANADA

The United States

The royal tour of Canada was announced ten weeks before the royal wedding, so it was quite a surprise when the additional two-day visit to California was announced on 4 May, just five days after the Westminster Abbey ceremony. The news spread like wildfire "across the pond". The special relationship between the United States and the British royal family has always been strong and US film crews and photographers made up highest number of overseas media in London for the wedding.

LEFT: *The Duke and Duchess of Cool. Catherine and William's relaxed style and engaging warmth charmed America during their brief visit. Here they arrive at the Santa Barbara Polo and Racquet Club in California for a charity polo match on the second day of their visit.*

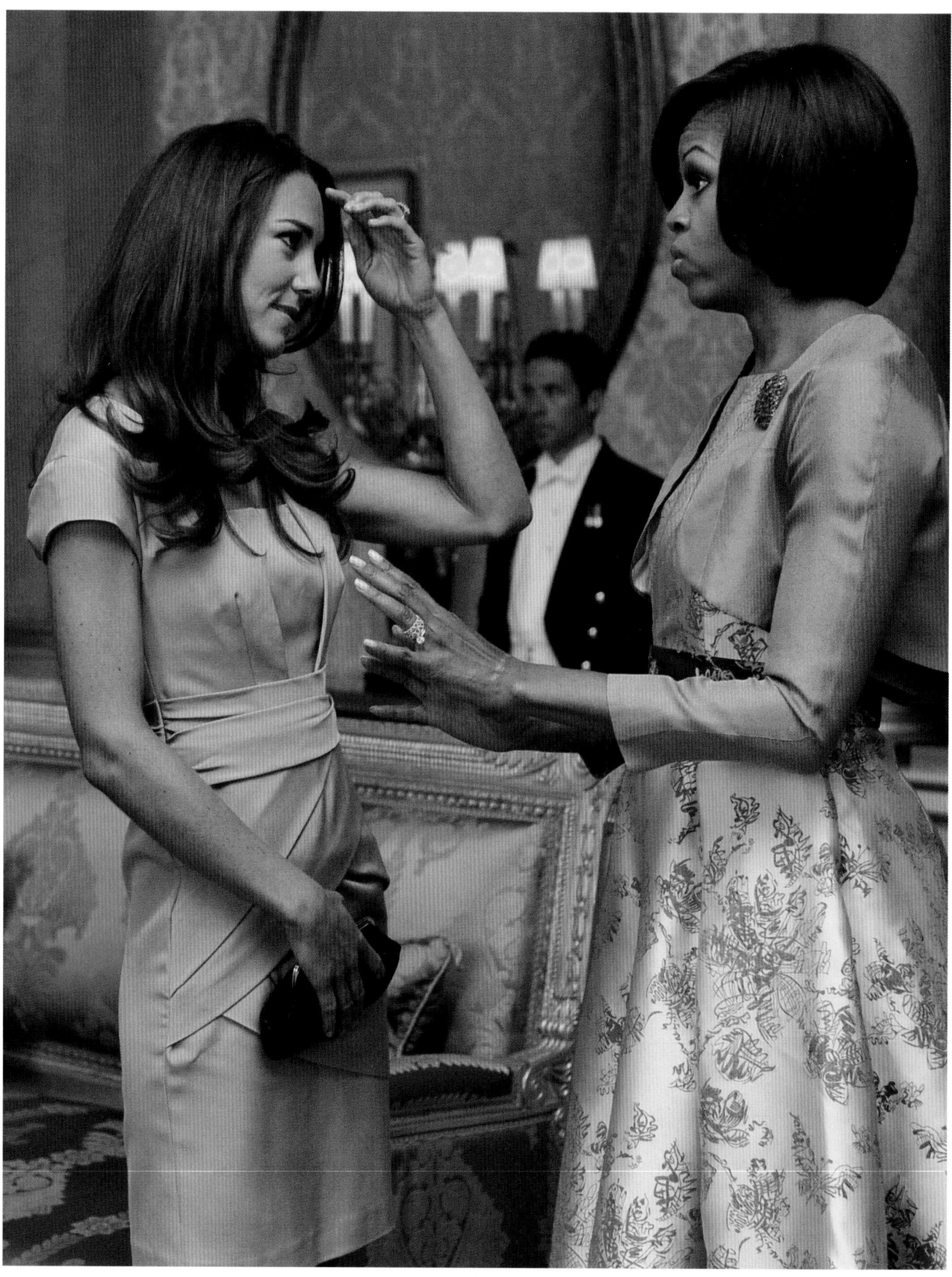

America had, after all, fallen in love with William's mother. Charles and Diana's 1985 visit to Washington sparked off royal fever, particularly when the princess took to the dance floor at the White House with her teenage idol, John Travolta. After the royal couple's divorce in 1996 it was widely rumoured that Diana would set up home in the US and one of her final public engagements was to attend a reception at Christie's in New York before the sale of her couture suits and gowns – the brainchild of Prince William – which raised millions of dollars for charity.

While Kate had never been to the United States before this visit, William had paid several private visits. In August 1992 Princess Diana took William, aged 11, and his eight-year-old brother Harry for a ten-day holiday in Florida so they could enjoy the delights of Disney World while staying at the Grand Floridian

LEFT: *Two of the world's most famous women meet at last. Catherine talks to US First Lady Michelle Obama during a private meeting at Buckingham Palace on 24 May 2011.*

BELOW: *A special relationship. The Queen poses for the camera with the 12th US President of her reign while their consorts enjoy a joke before the official State Banquet at Buckingham Palace.*

Hotel. Two hours after their arrival at Orlando they were spotted hurtling down Splash Mountain as well as venturing on to the Big Thunder Mountain Railroad and the Jungle Cruise. The next day they headed for the Disney-MGM Studios Theme Park where William wanted to see the *Indiana Jones* Epic Stunt Spectacular. Three years later the princess and her sons returned to the US for another break. This time they stayed at the holiday home of actress Goldie Hawn in Aspen and Diana took the princes white-water rafting on the Colorado River.

Before the visit in July 2011, the prince's most recent break in America was in August 2004 when he visited Nashville to stay with 22-year-old Anna Sloan, a university friend. Dubbed "Tennessee William" by the local press, the prince, according to *People* magazine, "swam in the pool and mostly socialized in the house". There were brief excursions into town when William bought a pair of Abercrombie and Fitch blue jeans for $69.50 and a meal at upmarket restaurant Sperry's, where the party of 15 split the $600 tab and, according to *People*, staff said that William "left a good tip".

At 3.59pm on 9 July, William and Kate landed in Los Angeles and looked happy and relaxed as they walked down the steps of the Canadian Air Force Airbus. Kate wore a lavender Peridot dress by Serbian-born Roksanda Illinic, a perfect choice for

ABOVE: *William and Catherine touch down on American soil as they arrive at Los Angeles airport for a three-day visit. It was Catherine's first visit to the USA.*

RIGHT: *William and Kate arrive for a private reception at the Los Angeles home of the British Consul-General, Dame Barbara Hay (standing on the right of the couple). The Duchess looks cool and elegant in a lavender dress.*

the heat wave that greeted their arrival. As she touched American soil for the first time in her life the Duchess was handed a red, white and blue bouquet, a reminder of the flags of both the United Kingdom and the United States.

There would be no rafting or Disney characters during this visit. They were there to attend a UK Trade and Investment-sponsored meeting to promote British technological business in America. Within minutes of landing, the couple were whisked off with an LAPD escort to the Beverley Hilton where a crowd of 200 screaming fans welcomed them.

Afterwards William and Kate were driven to the British Consul's residence in Haydock Park – their home for the two-night stay. Here the couple attended a garden party and mingled with Los Angeles's finest, including former England football captain – and royal wedding guest – David Beckham and the head of Disney, Bob Iger. Once again Kate made a diplomatic choice when it came to her fashion, appearing in a "Maja" green silk dress by American couturier Diane Von Furstenberg, with a bag by the same designer.

BELOW: *The royal couple look happy and relaxed as they enjoy a joke during their first engagement in California. They are attending the dauntingly named UK Trade & Investment and Variety's Venture Capital and New Media Summit reception at the Beverly Hilton Hotel.*

ABOVE: *The royal couple pose for photos with guests at a reception hosted by the Consul-General, Dame Barbara Hay, at her Los Angeles residence. Before greeting the 200 invitees Kate changed into an elegant green silk dress by American designer Diane Von Furstenberg.*

With only 48 hours in California and a tight schedule, the couple had to turn down many invitations, including one from Homer Simpson. According to *Entertainment Weekly*, the producers of *The Simpsons* heard the prince was a fan and so Homer wrote a "frosting-stained-yet-surprisingly-eloquent letter to William and Kate" requesting a royal visit, adding, "We know your vacation time is precious, and you must be very tired from your busy schedule back home of jousting and fighting dragons." After a polite refusal from Clarence House, the show's executive producer, Al Jean, said: "Our next choice is Prince Harry, and then we'll go to one of Fergie's kids."

The day after their arrival the couple flew by helicopter to Santa Barbara for a charity polo match at the Polo & Racquet Club. Celebrities, including actors Rob Lowe, Zoe Saldana, Billy Zane and Joe Jonas, were among those paying up to $4,000 a ticket to rub shoulders with William and Kate (and $60,000 to play opposite the prince in the match). The event raised over $5 million for the American Friends of The Foundation of Prince William and Prince Harry.

Kate, dressed in a silver and marble-grey hand-painted chinoiserie silk dress by Jenny Packham, delighted guests and, crucially, the photographers by presenting a trophy to her husband and kissing him on both cheeks. As with so many other aspects of this tour, comparisons were made with William's parents. Photos were unearthed of Charles and Diana kissing on the lips during similar polo presentations at Smith's Lawn near Windsor in the 1980s and, of course, the famous "missed kiss" in Jaipur, India, in 1992 when Charles attempted to kiss his wife and she tilted her head so he ended up kissing her neck, a visible sign of the deteriorating state of their marriage.

The highlight of the US visit was a dinner hosted by the British Academy of Film and Television Arts at the Belasco Theater in downtown Los Angeles. William is President of BAFTA and was there to introduce film studio executives

BELOW: *William was warmly greeted by David Beckham, who had attended the royal wedding in April. The football legend delivered several signed LA Galaxy shirts for William to auction at one if his charities. His wife, who was due to give birth to their daughter a few days later, was unable to be present.*

RIGHT: *Kate stepped out in a stylish floral knee-length Jenny Packham dress with taupe sandals when she accompanied William to a charity polo match held at the Santa Barbara Racquet and Polo Club on 9 July.*

to 42 "Brits to Watch" – actors, producers and animators chosen by a panel of experts as best representing the up-and-coming talent of UK film, television and video games. Among the 42 was actress Jessica Brown-Findlay, who stars as Lady Sybil Crawley in ITV's *Downton Abbey* and who discovered the couple are huge fans of the award-winning costume drama.

In a speech to movie executives, William asked: "Please give them the opportunities you have always extended to some of the brightest and best that Britain has to offer. When American and British creative talent gets together magic happens."

Hollywood's finest paid $25,000 per table to break bread with the royals and clearly thought it was money well spent. Actress Nicole Kidman, who sat at the couple's table, said: "They make me smile, I love them." Kidman and legendary singer Barbra Streisand, a favourite of William's father, held their hands out to be shaken across the table and Jennifer Lopez was spotted whooping with delight after being introduced.

ABOVE: *Catherine poses with William's victorious polo team after presenting them with their cup. The event was in aid of the American Friends of the Foundation of Prince William and Prince Harry, a charity which supports disadvantaged children, conservation causes and military veterans and their families.*

Actor Jason Bateman seemed overwhelmed when he told reporters: "They are the ultimate movie stars. We're all just kind of faking it and getting paid for it. They are the real deal." Britain's Stephen Fry, a guest at both the BAFTA dinner and the previous evening's reception, summed up the adulation: "If you brought back Clark Gable and Marilyn Monroe to life, Americans couldn't be more excited than they are by the presence of the Cambridges."

On the final morning of their tour, the couple attended a reception for US patrons of Tusk Trust, a conservation charity supported by William. They also visited Inner City Arts, a performance-art centre for deprived youths.

As throughout their whole tour of Canada and the US, the couple proved hands-on and competitive. In this case they both had a go at painting – William attempting to create a box on canvas and Catherine a snail. At the same time there was plenty of banter between them, with Catherine at one point asking her husband: "William, do you know what you're doing? Start from the centre."

Their last point of call was a job fair called "Hiring Our Heroes" for returning troops, featuring employers such as Mattel, Wal-Mart, Warner Brothers and CBS. Talking of The Foundation of Prince William and Prince Harry during his speech,

BELOW: *Royal déjà vu. During their 1985 visit to the USA, William's mother, Diana, Princess of Wales, presented the prizes after a charity match in Palm Beach, Florida in which Prince Charles took part.*

EXPRESS

William provoked laughter by having a dig at his brother, a military helicopter pilot, referring to him as "Harry, my low-flying Apache, very average brother".

The visit had a real impact on the guests. Kelly York, a 23-year-old Air Force veteran looking for a job, said: "I'm sure that they had 50 million places they could go and see. The fact that they even take five minutes to stop here and say something to the veterans, that's huge."

After this the couple drove to the airport where they boarded a British Airways scheduled flight for London. They had dazzled California and reinvigorated the ties between the monarchy and Canada. As they took off they must have had the satisfaction of knowing their first joint tour was, for everyone, a job well done.

LEFT: *William scored four goals for his victorious team. Kate presented each competitor with a blue Tiffany & Co box with a white ribbon, and when the crowd chanted "kiss" she happily obliged.*

BELOW: *William, as President of the British Academy of Film and Television Arts, attended the 2011 BAFTA Brits To Watch event at the Belasco Theater on 9 July 2011. Catherine looks effortlessly stylish in an Alexander McQueen gown and diamond earrings loaned to her by Queen Elizabeth.*

ABOVE: *On the final day of their US visit, the royal couple visited the Inner-City Arts Center in Los Angeles and were very much hands-on. Here Catherine laughs as William teases her about the huge red snail she has painted.*

RIGHT: *Later in the day they attended a job fair for ex-servicemen where they helped prepare care packages for the children of military personnel.*

FAR RIGHT: *Kate wears one of her favourite colour combinations – navy and cream – both designed by one of her favourite retailers, Whistles, as the couple say goodbye to the US at Los Angeles international airport at the end of their three-day stay in California.*

ON DUTY

William and Catherine's working life is centred around the office they share with Prince Harry in St James's Palace. In January 2009 the Queen granted her two grandsons a joint Royal Household which, according to a Palace press release, "lays the basis for the princes' lives in the future as they progress their public, military and charitable activities". Since the royal wedding, it has expanded to include Catherine's public role as a member of the royal family.

LEFT: *Catherine presenting service medals to members of the Irish Guards at the Victoria Barracks in Windsor on 25 June 2011. The Queen made William a Colonel of the Irish Guards two months before his wedding.*

The head of the Household is Jamie Lowther-Pinkerton, William's most trusted aide. The former SAS officer is distantly related to the princes, all of them being descended from William Ponsonby, 1st Viscount Duncannon, an ancestor of the late Queen Mother, to whom Lowther-Pinkerton was an equerry for the period 1984–86. After that he was handpicked by the then Prime Minister, Margaret Thatcher, to lead two major SAS counter-narcotics operations against the drug lords of Colombia in 1989. Five years later he was part of a specialist SAS operation in Bosnia.

Lowther-Pinkerton returned to royal service in March 2005 when Prince Charles interviewed him for the post of Private Secretary. He lives in Suffolk with his wife Susannah and their four children. One of his sons, William, was a pageboy at the royal wedding.

The royal couple's private diary is organized by Helen Asprey, a scion of the jewellery family, who has been William's personal assistant since 2000. Before that she worked in the Duke of Edinburgh's office at Buckingham Palace. She deals with the private correspondence of William, Catherine and Harry as well as co-ordinating their private diaries and overseeing holidays and weekends away.

The staff also includes their public relations chief, Miguel Head, a former career diplomat on secondment from the Foreign Office, who was very much responsible for the smooth running of the 2011 North American tour. In addition, in 2009 the Queen appointed Sir David Manning, the former British Ambassador to the USA, in a part-time advisory role to the princes and their Household.

At present Catherine doesn't have a lady-in-waiting, essential for any royal lady in the past but now largely ignored in the working lives of Camilla, Duchess of Cornwall and Sophie Wessex. On occasions Helen Asprey has stood in as an assistant to Catherine, notably when the latter went to visit Westminster Abbey before confirming it as the wedding venue.

In her post-divorce years, Diana occasionally asked her sister Sarah McCorquodale to accompany her on royal engagements, and it is conceivable that Pippa Middleton could accept a similar role in Catherine's life. However, given the media circus that accompanies either sister whenever they appear in public, it is unlikely royal advisors would be happy with Pippa joining the team.

Two royal in-laws have helped ease Catherine's transition to royal life. She is particularly close to William's stepmother Camilla. The two met for lunch in Koffman's restaurant at the Berkeley Hotel in Knightsbridge in the run-up to the wedding, where the Duchess of Cornwall was overheard by a fellow diner saying, "If I can give you one bit of advice…".

That "bit of advice" may well have been for Catherine to try to preserve some of her own identity in her new life. Camilla has kept on her former home, Ray Mill House at Laycock in Wiltshire, as a bolt hole where she can be totally her old self. She has set aside one day a week to play grandma to her

ABOVE: *Jamie Lowther-Pinkerton (Prince William and Prince Harry's Private Secretary) attends the annual Chelsea Pensioners Founders' Day Parade on 9 June 2011 at the Royal Hospital, Chelsea, in southwest London.*

RIGHT: *The Duke and Duchess both look glamorous as they attend the 10th Annual Absolute Return for Kids (ARK) gala dinner on behalf of the Foundation of Prince William and Prince Harry, at Perks Field, Kensington Palace, on 9 June 2011.*

OPPOSITE: *Catherine, Duchess of Cambridge makes her way down the Mall during the Trooping the Colour procession.*

BELOW: *Soldiers escort Queen Elizabeth II up the Mall following the Trooping the Colour ceremony on 11 June 2011. More than 600 guardsmen and cavalry make up the parade. The Trooping the Colour is believed to have first been performed during the reign of King Charles II. In 1748, it was decided that the parade would be used to mark the official birthday of the sovereign. Queen Elizabeth's actual birthday is on 21 April.*

five grandchildren – two by her son Tom and three by his sister Laura. She also goes on what she calls her "bucket and spade" holidays each summer with her children and their families.

William reportedly asked his aunt, Sophie Wessex, to take Catherine under her wing and pass on advice, so that his wife was more prepared for her role than his mother had been. Diana was almost a decade younger than Catherine when she married into the royal family and would later complain that she had been thrown in at the deep end and given little training. Sophie has faced several challenges, from a potentially life-threatening ectopic pregnancy in December 2001 to the premature birth of her daughter Louise which involved a placental abruption that put both mother and daughter's lives at risk.

Sophie tried to juggle both her royal life with running her own public relations company. This led to a conflict of interest, most famously when a potential client turned out to be an undercover reporter from a tabloid newspaper. The Countess was recorded making several unflattering comments about members of the government as well as her royal relations, and appeared to be abusing her royal status to gain clients. The following year both she and Prince Edward abandoned

their careers to concentrate on royal duties. It was a painful but invaluable lesson, and one she would have wanted to share with Catherine.

It was no doubt with the lessons of Camilla, Sophie and, particularly, Diana in mind that William and Catherine's public engagements have been limited and tightly controlled. Before the trip to Canada and the USA there were only a handful of appearances, although each in its own way was significant.

Their first royal duty as a married couple was a diplomatic one. On 24 May they met US President Barack Obama and his wife Michelle at Buckingham Palace on the first day of their state visit to the UK. The newlyweds greeted the Obamas in the opulent 1844 Room, designed for the state visit of Emperor Nicholas I of Russia as guest of Queen Victoria. The meeting took place just a few days after William and Catherine had returned from their Seychelles honeymoon and they both looked relaxed as they spent 20 minutes or so with the visitors. No TV cameras or reporters were in the room but it's likely that they talked about the royal wedding and the forthcoming royal visit to California.

It had been widely speculated that one or both of the Obamas would be invited to the Westminster Abbey ceremony, following in the footsteps of Nancy Reagan who represented her husband Ronald at the 1981 wedding of Charles and Diana. William and Catherine's wedding was not, however, a state occasion,

ABOVE & RIGHT: *Following Trooping the Colour the royal family normally gathers on the palace balcony for the traditional flypast to honour the Queen's birthday. Here Catherine and William are joined by the Earl and Countess of Wessex and their daughter Lady Louise Windsor as they watch the spectacular Red Arrows fly over in formation.*

so only royalty and Commonwealth leaders were invited. The palace meeting was seen as intending to offset any criticism that the Obamas had been snubbed by not being invited to the royal wedding.

On 9 June the Cambridges made their first public appearance as a married couple when they attended a lavish gala dinner in a pavilion in the grounds of Kensington Palace, William's childhood home. They were there to mark the tenth anniversary of the Absolute Return for Kids (ARK) charity and shared a table with 24 other famous faces, including Baron de Rothschild, socialite Jemima Khan, actor Colin Firth, fashion designer Tom Ford and Prince Pavlos of Greece and his wife Marie Chantal. Catherine looked fabulous in a floor-length rose pink, sequinned, organza Jenny Packham evening gown, which retails at £3,835, and matching LK Bennett shoes costing £175.

Addressing the audience at the dinner, William said: "My brother, Catherine and I hope to use our philanthropy as a long-term catalyst for meaningful change." Part of the entertainment enjoyed by the guests was a team of Mexican

divers performing in a specially prepared pool. William joked that he would have an interesting time explaining the events of the evening to the Queen. He said: "I would like to share with you the conversation I am going to have with my grandmother tomorrow as I try and describe this; the swimming pool outside and the men wearing the most tight Speedos I have ever seen in my life."

There were no Speedos in sight at Catherine's next royal engagement two days later, when she attended one of the key ceremonies of the royal year: Trooping the Colour. The Duchess shared a barouche with Camilla for the journey from Buckingham Palace to Horse Guards Parade, where she watched her husband arrive on horseback as part of the Queen's escort. Afterwards Catherine made her first appearance on the balcony of Buckingham Palace since the wedding day six weeks earlier.

On the Monday following Trooping the Colour, Catherine was in Windsor Castle for the annual Garter Service, where once again she was an onlooker as Prince William took centre stage. This time the prince was in the procession of Garter Knights and walked ahead of his grandmother from the State Apartments and into the Lower Ward of the castle precincts. Catherine watched with Camilla from the Galilee Porch entrance to the chapel and made him blush as she caught his eye and beamed at him.

The couple's final appearance before leaving for Canada was at Victoria Barracks in Windsor, where Catherine and the prince handed out operational medals to members of the Irish Guards. The soldiers on parade had recently returned from service in Afghanistan. William had been made the regiment's colonel earlier in the year and wore his Irish Guards' uniform at his wedding. William spoke of his "pride and humility" in being there and a royal aide said the Duchess was pleased to be presenting the medals to a regiment "so close to her husband's heart".

OPPOSITE: *Prince William walks in the procession of Garter Knights behind his uncle Prince Edward as they arrive for the Garter Service at St George's Chapel in Windsor Castle on 13 June 2011. The Order is the oldest order of chivalry in Britain and William was created the 1,000th knight in 2008 by his grandmother, the Queen.*

ABOVE: *The knights return to the State Apartments in open-top landaus. Here William and Catherine share a carriage with Prince Charles and the Duchess of Cornwall as they leave the service.*

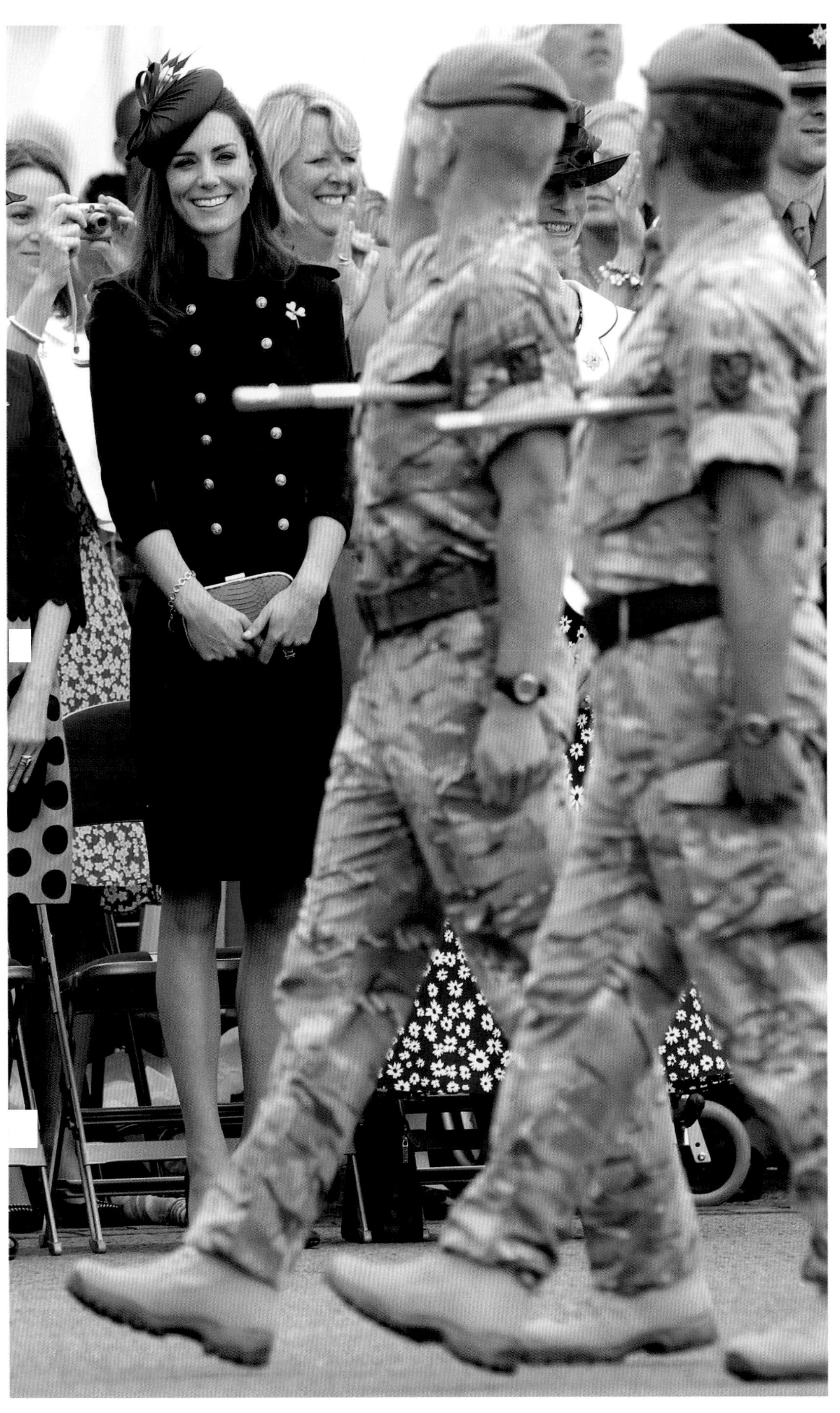

LEFT: *Catherine, smiles as she is saluted during the Irish Guards' medal parade at the Victoria Barracks on 25 June 2011 in Windsor.*

RIGHT: *The royal couple arrive for the ceremony at Windsor Barracks. The prince wears an Irish Guards frock coat. Catherine opted for a military chic look, wearing a navy double-breasted knee-length coat with brass buttons and epaulettes.*

PRIVATE LIFE

During her first royal summer the new Duchess of Cambridge proved she could be just as much the centre of attention at private events as she is at public ones.

LEFT: *The hands give it away as William, Harry and Catherine all look self-conscious as they arrive for the Investec Derby Day at Epsom Downs Racecourse on 4 June 2011.*

William, Catherine and Harry were surprise guests at the Epsom Derby on 4 June 2011, where they joined other family members in cheering on the Queen's horse. In 1953, the year of her coronation, the Queen's horse Aureole came second at the Derby but, having faithfully attended this prestigious race ever since, the ultimate accolade of owing the winner of the Derby has always eluded her. Finally, in 2011, she had her strongest chance in years when Carlton House was declared fit to run and started the race as the hot favourite. The royal family came out in force to support the Queen, with four of her grandchildren – William, Harry, Beatrice and Eugenie – present, as well as Prince Andrew and the Earl and Countess of Wessex. Sadly Her Majesty's dream was shattered and Pour Moi romped home to win.

With the sun beating down on the racecourse, Catherine looked cool and summery in her floaty white Reiss dress. Known as the Peacock, it, like many of her other high-street buys, sold out almost immediately after she was seen wearing it. Catherine teamed her outfit with a jacket by Joseph, together with nude LK Bennett shoes and a matching clutch bag. It was the Duchess's second Reiss outfit in less than a fortnight, her first being the £175 dress she

BELOW: *Michael and Carole Middleton arrive in the royal carriage procession as they attend Ladies Day on the third day of the Royal Ascot meeting: 16 June 2011.*

RIGHT: *Pippa Middleton and Catherine attend the wedding of Sam Waley-Cohen and Annabel Ballin at St Michael and All Angels Church on 11 June in Lambourn, Berkshire, near the Middletons' home.*

ABOVE: *A 62-gun salute is fired in honour of the ninetieth birthday of Prince Philip, the Duke of Edinburgh, near Tower Bridge on 10 June 2011. Prince Philip, the plain-speaking husband of Queen Elizabeth II, said he was "winding down" his royal workload as he marked his ninetieth birthday with a typical lack of fuss. The gruff patriarch, the longest-serving consort in British history, spent his birthday at work, hosting a charity reception and chairing a conference for military colonels, but admitted that he would now take a step back.*

wore to meet the Obamas at Buckingham Palace.

Later in the month she wore a stunning £795 Alice Temperley dress, again teamed with LK Bennett nude court shoes, when she and William watched Andy Murray play Frenchman Richard Gasquet on Centre Court at Wimbledon.

Afterwards the victorious Scot met the royal couple, who congratulated him and gave him a pat on the back. Murray later told journalists: "If I'd known they were coming, I would have shaved. I was thinking to myself as I came off I was sweaty and very hairy. I said to them, 'I'm sorry, I'm a bit sweaty.' But it was very nice to get to meet them."

Also in June, Catherine attended the first of three summer weddings. Just hours after witnessing her first Trooping the Colour, the Duchess zoomed down the M4 to join sister Pippa at the marriage of jockey Sam Waley-Cohen to party organizer Annabel Ballin at St Michael and All Angels Church in Lambourn, Berkshire. Sam was widely credited with saving William and Catherine's romance: stories circulated that he helped the couple rekindle their romance following their split in 2007 – a claim he has since modestly denied.

Catherine followed the traditional royal example of not upstaging the bride by wearing something new. Her hat was the same one she'd worn at that morning's ceremony and her dress was the spot-pattern black-and-white one she'd first been photographed wearing at Boujis nightclub in London in 2007.

Catherine drove herself to the wedding and she and Pippa were seen chatting to wedding guests and some of the onlookers outside the church.

Afterwards the sisters joined others in making an avenue outside the church for the newlyweds to walk through.

On 25 September 2011 William and Catherine were both present for the wedding of their close friends Harriet Colthurst and Thomas Sutton at Wilton in Wiltshire. The prince arrived early to fulfil his duties as an usher and Catherine arrived with another friend, Louise Aubrey-Fletcher. The Duchess wore a mid-length raspberry-coloured lace dress by Collette Dinnigan with a matching pillbox hat and Prada pumps. It later emerged that the dress had first been worn by Carole Middleton at the Royal Academy's Summer Exhibition in 2009.

There was more royal clothes-recycling for the wedding of William's cousin Zara Phillips to England rugby player Mike Tindall at Canongate Kirk on 31 July. The evening before the wedding, Catherine joined other royal guests and friends for a reception on the Royal Yacht *Britannia*, and chose to wear the green Diane Von Furstenberg dress she had first worn on her visit to Los Angeles earlier in the month.

For the following day's wedding she opted for something far older, a pale-gold dress she had worn for the 2006 wedding of Camilla's daughter, Laura Parker Bowles, at St Cyriac's Church in Lacock, Wiltshire. On this occasion Catherine

BELOW: *Queen Elizabeth II and Prince Philip pose with the Dean of Windsor, Reverend David Conner, after a church service at St George's Chapel, Windsor to mark Prince Philip's ninetieth birthday.*

wore a dramatic tilted hat instead of the fascinator she had worn in 2006. On her feet she wore her by-now trademark nude pumps.

Another favourite outfit made a second appearance at the Thanksgiving Service at St George's Chapel, Windsor Castle to mark Prince Philip's ninetieth birthday. Catherine, again, didn't want to be accused of snatching headlines by wearing something dazzlingly new, so chose a pale-blue jacquard coat dress bought for the 2009 wedding of William's friend Nicholas van Cutsem to Alice Hadden-Paton at Wellington Barracks. More mother–daughter sharing emerged as the jaunty blue Jane Corbett fascinator Catherine teamed with the blue jacquard dress on this occasion had also been worn by Carole Middleton at Royal Ascot in June 2010.

Earlier in 2011 it had been reported by the press that the Duchess told a friend she didn't want to be a "clothes horse" and that she intended to wear her outfits again and again. She was quoted as reportedly saying: "Times are tough; I cannot be expected to wear a new outfit for every royal engagement. I am not a fashion model."

BELOW: *The Duke and Duchess of Cambridge talk with the Dean of Windsor, Reverend David Conner, after the church service held two days after Prince Philip's ninetieth birthday.*

RIGHT, ABOVE: *With former tennis champion Billie Jean King (in black) in the row behind, Catherine and William attend the fourth-round match between Andy Murray of Great Britain and Richard Gasquet of France on day seven of the Wimbledon Lawn Tennis Championships at the All England Lawn Tennis and Croquet Club on 27 June.*

RIGHT, BELOW: *The parents and sister of the Duchess of Cambridge – Carole and Michael Middleton and Pippa Middleton, accompanied by Pippa's then boyfriend Alex Loudon – attend the men's singles quarter-final match between Swiss player Roger Federer and Frenchman Jo-Wilfried Tsonga at the Wimbledon Tennis Championships on 29 June.*

LEFT: *William and Catherine attend Zara Phillips and Mike Tindall's pre-wedding party on the royal yacht* Britannia *on 29 July 2011 at Leith, near Edinburgh.*

RIGHT: *The Duchess of Cambridge arrives for the wedding of Zara Phillips and Mike Tindall at Canongate Kirk in Edinburgh, 30 July 2011.*

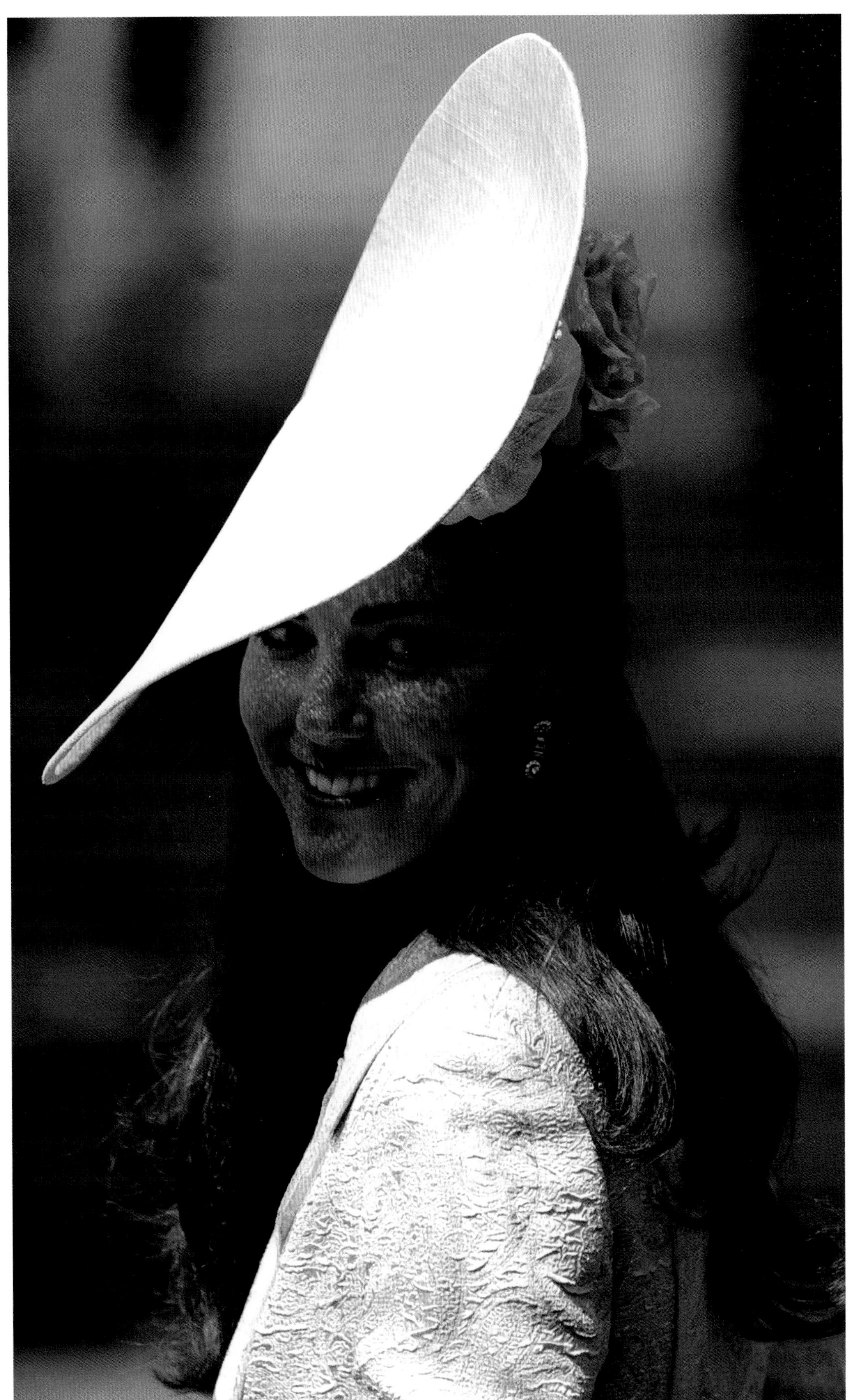

LEFT & RIGHT: *England rugby player Mike Tindall with his new wife Zara Phillips, the Queen's eldest grandchild, after their wedding at Canongate Kirk in Edinburgh on 30 July 2011.*

In the course of the service at Windsor Castle the Dean made the audience laugh by telling them the Duke "doesn't like to the praised" and described him as a "modest" man. Later there was a reception for guests in St George's Hall and the Grand Reception Room, Windsor Castle, ahead of a private family lunch.

During the summer it was revealed that Catherine, like Diana and other royal wives, had been having training by the SAS in emergency driving techniques in case of an ambush or terrorist incident. This is particularly important as the Duchess, as her mother-in-law does, likes to drive herself around London.

For their stays in the London area, William and Catherine were based at Nottingham Cottage, a small detached house in the grounds of Kensington Palace which had once been home to the Queen's governess, Marion Crawford. Later it was announced that they would take over Apartment 1a, Kensington Palace, the former home of William's great-aunt, Princess Margaret, and near the Waleses' apartment where he was brought up with Harry. The lavish four-storey home is protected by a walled garden and will offer the couple much-needed privacy in the capital. The couple are expected to move in after refurbishment is completed in 2013.

The Royal

CHARITABLE ENTERPRISES

Following their tour of North America, it was announced that William and Catherine would be scaling down their royal engagements partly because, according to a spokesperson for the Palace, "they are very conscious to make sure that the run-up to 2012 is the Queen's year", but also so William could resume his career and Catherine could spend time investigating the charities she wished to be associated with.

LEFT: *Catherine meets members of staff during a walkabout after opening the new Oak Centre for Children and Young People at Royal Marsden Hospital on 29 September 2011 in Sutton, Surrey.*

Nevertheless the couple made several appearances to support causes that were close to both their hearts, from visiting the Royal Marsden Hospital to supporting an appeal for the National Memorial Arboretum. Also during this time Catherine carried out her first solo engagement.

One of the key roles of the royal family is to reflect the nation's compassion during times of crisis, be those natural disasters or human atrocities. In 1996 the Queen memorably shed a tear when she laid flowers outside the school at Dunblane in Scotland where 16 children and a teacher were killed, while in 2011 William represented his grandmother when he flew to New Zealand to meet grieving families and thank emergency services following the devastating earthquake that killed 181 people in Christchurch.

BELOW: *The Queen and Princess Anne arrive on 17 March 1996 with a member of the Scottish Office to lay a wreath at the entrance of Dunblane Primary School, where a gunman had shot 16 children and a teacher four days earlier.*

RIGHT: *William and Catherine walking with the Lord Mayor of Birmingham, Councillor Anita Ward, on a visit to riot-affected areas at Summerfield Community Centre, Birmingham, on 19 August 2011.*

ABOVE: *Meeting Ajay and Monika Bhatia on 19 August 2011 at the Machan Express coffee bar in the centre of Birmingham, which had been ransacked during that summer's riots in the area. The Duke and Duchess of Cambridge also met the parents of the men of South Asian descent who were killed in the riots when they were mown down by a car in the ethnically mixed Winson Green area of the city.*

On 19 August William and Catherine met those affected by the summer riots in the Winson Green area of Birmingham. They met the parents of three men who were killed when they were mown down by a car as they tried to protect shops and homes from looters. Meanwhile Prince Harry met fire fighters in Manchester and Prince Charles toured areas affected by the riots in London, including Tottenham where the violence began.

After their 20-minute private meeting at Summerfield Community Centre, William and Catherine met local people affected by the riots as well as those who had helped victims afterwards.

Mandy Sankey, nurse manager at Birmingham Children's Hospital, said the royal couple wanted to thank everyone for their hard work. She told reporters: "William said, 'We're sure you have already heard how grateful we are but we wanted to come here to say thank you in person.'"

Afterwards the Duke and Duchess drove to the city centre to visit the Machan Express coffee shop, which had lost £15,000 worth of stock during the riots but was still open for business the next day. William told the owner, Ajay Bhatia, "I am sorry this has happened to you."

Earlier, Derrick Campbell, a government adviser on anti-social behaviour and a community leader in Sandwell, said of the royal visit: "I think what came over really well was the human side to the royal family. It wasn't tokenistic, you could sense the genuine emotion that they showed and I think that really went a long way to reassuring us that these people really do care about what took place here."

At the end of September Catherine followed in Diana's footsteps by visiting the Royal Marsden Hospital in Surrey, where she and William, who is the hospital's president, opened the £18 million Oak Centre for Children and Young People. The Royal Marsden was especially important to the late Princess of Wales and it was here that she carried out her first solo engagement in 1982. She was also its president from 1989 until her death in 1997.

William and Catherine met young cancer sufferers and the prince took off his jacket and rolled up his sleeves to create the informal tone that characterized their visit. He posed for a photo with seven-year-old Ellis Andrews, who was

BELOW: *Charles and Camilla pose with volunteers from the Youth United network at the Croydon Voluntary Action Centre on 17 August 2011. They met residents and families whose homes and businesses were affected by the outbreaks of rioting and looting in the Croydon area.*

waiting for a bone-marrow transplant, while the Duchess chatted to Fabian Bate, aged nine, who was in the middle of four hours of chemotherapy.

A few weeks after the visit it emerged that Catherine had written a letter to Fabian, with whom she'd chatted for some time during her visit. The typed letter, which was signed "Catherine", said how much she had enjoyed meeting him and that she was "touched by his strength of character" and delighted to hear that one of his sisters was able to donate bone marrow to help him. She added, "I will keep my fingers crossed that your health goes from strength to strength in the coming months" and promised to keep him "in my thoughts and prayers".

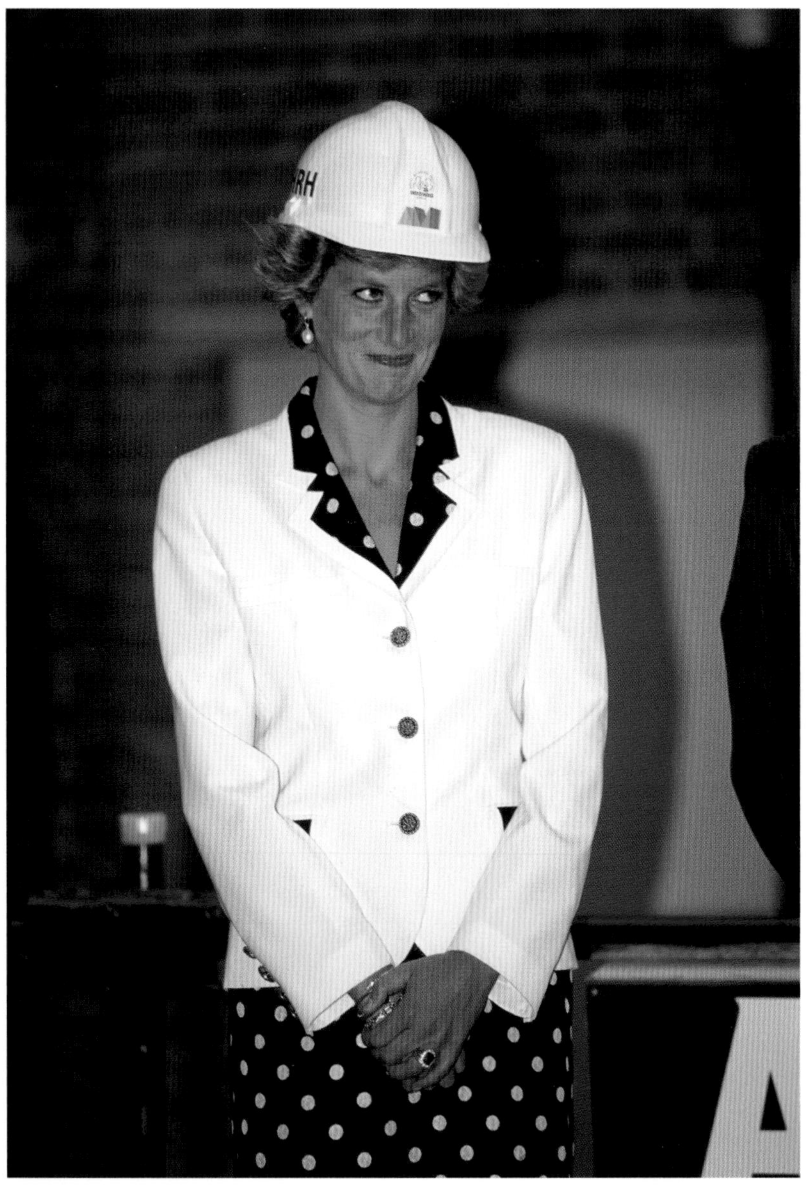

LEFT: *Princess Diana (1961–97) wearing a Paul Costelloe suit and a hard hat at a topping-out ceremony at the Royal Marsden Hospital, London, June 1990.*

RIGHT, ABOVE: *William and Catherine meeting patient Digby Davidson, 14, as they open a children's cancer unit at the Royal Marsden Hospital in Sutton, Surrey, on 29 September 2011.*

RIGHT, BELOW: *The Duke and Duchess of Cambridge officially open the new Oak Centre for Children and Young People at the Royal Marsden Hospital on 29 September 2011.*

FOLLOWING PAGES, LEFT: *William poses with seven-year-old patient Ellis Andrews in the children's cancer unit of the Royal Marsden Hospital.*

FOLLOWING PAGES, RIGHT: *Catherine, Duchess of Cambridge speaks to guests at an event in support of the "In Kind Direct" charity at Clarence House, London on 26 October 2011. The event was her first solo engagement.*

WORLDWIDE
FREERIDE

The ROYAL MARSDEN
TRH The Duke and Duchess of Cambridge
opened The Oak Centre for Children and Young People
on 29 September 2011
The original Wolfson Children and Adolescent Unit was opened by
HRH The Princess of Wales on 25 February 1993

Toilet
Toilet

Before the Royal Marsden visit, William, who had been up all night on a search and rescue mission, was quoted in the press as joking: "It was a bit of an early morning," before adding, "It's great to be here finally – we've been talking about this for a while." For the visit Catherine wore a sculpted £450 Amanda Wakeley oatmeal felt dress with three-quarter-length sleeves and her favourite LK Bennett nude high heels and matching clutch bag.

By now Catherine must have been aware that for those marrying into the royal family charity dinners are a regular occurrence. The Duchess attended several during the autumn. In October she looked stunning in a red Beulah London evening gown at a fundraiser held at St James's Palace, organized by 100 Women in Hedge Funds. The event raised more than £675,000 for the Child Bereavement Charity, also an organization William is associated with.

On 10 November, the royal couple attended another dinner at St James's Palace, this time in aid of the National Memorial Arboretum Future Foundations Appeal, of which William is a patron. Catherine looked stunning in a silver Grecian-style gown designed by Jenny Packham, which was draped over one shoulder and gathered in at the waist. The addition of a bright red poppy, the emblem of Remembrance Day, added a dash of colour.

ABOVE & RIGHT: *Attending a dinner reception in aid of the National Memorial Arboretum Appeal at St James's Palace in London, on 10 November 2011. The Appeal was launched in April 2009 by its patron, the Duke of Cambridge, to develop the Arboretum into a world-renowned centre for remembrance and to improve facilities for the 300,000 visiting families, servicemen and women, veterans and members of the public each year.*

The dinner that made the most headlines was on 20 October when Catherine carried out her first solo engagement. She stood in for her father-in-law, Prince Charles, at short notice after the prince was suddenly required to fly to Saudi Arabia to present the Queen's condolences following the death of the Saudi Crown Prince.

The black-tie event was held at Clarence House for the charity In Kind Direct, which Charles founded in 1996 and which redistributes surplus goods from manufacturers and retailers to UK charities working both domestically and abroad. Catherine, dressed in an Amanda Wakeley gown, looked relaxed as she chatted to the 30 guests in the Garden Room before taking them through to dinner.

For once it wasn't Catherine's fashion that made headlines the next day but the fact that her swept-back hair revealed a seven-centimetre (three-inch) scar on her left temple, the result of a childhood operation. By chance, William has one in the same place, which he calls his Harry Potter scar, that was caused when a school friend accidentally hit him with a golf club.

In a statement released following the dinner, Catherine's spokesperson said: "She was so pleased that her first solo engagement was for the Prince of Wales, who has shown her so much support over the years." Robin Boles, the charity's chief executive, said Catherine was "completely natural, professional and charmed everyone. She spoke to every single guest and was genuinely interested in continuing to help."

CHRISTMAS & NEW YEAR 2011

The end of 2011 saw Catherine taking part for the first time in two of the events on the royal calendar for the Queen and her family. The first was Remembrance Day, when the monarch leads the nation's remembrance for all those who have given their lives fighting for their country.

LEFT: *Prince William, Prince Charles, Catherine, Camilla and Prince Harry walk to Sandringham Church for the traditional Christmas Day service on 25 December 2011. The Queen and the Duke of Edinburgh traditionally lead the royals in attending a church service at Sandringham Church on Christmas Day, but Prince Philip was in hospital. It was the Duchess of Cambridge's first Christmas at Sandringham after her marriage.*

The second was Christmas Day, traditionally celebrated by the royal family at Sandringham House in Norfolk, where three generations attend a service at St Mary Magdalene Church.

Also in autumn 2011 Catherine had her first overseas meeting with another royal family when she and the prince flew to Denmark for a charity event attended by Danish Crown Prince Frederik and his wife Princess Mary. The main purpose of the Danish visit on 2 November was to visit a UNICEF (United Nations Children's Fund) distribution centre in Copenhagen for East Africa famine relief. William and Catherine flew to the Danish capital and were met at the airport by Nicholas Archer, the British Ambassador, before they drove to Frederick VIII Palace for lunch with the Crown Prince and his wife. The two

BELOW: *Prince William, Catherine, Crown Prince Frederik of Denmark and Crown Princess Mary of Denmark visit the UNICEF Centre on 2 November 2011 in Copenhagen, Denmark.*

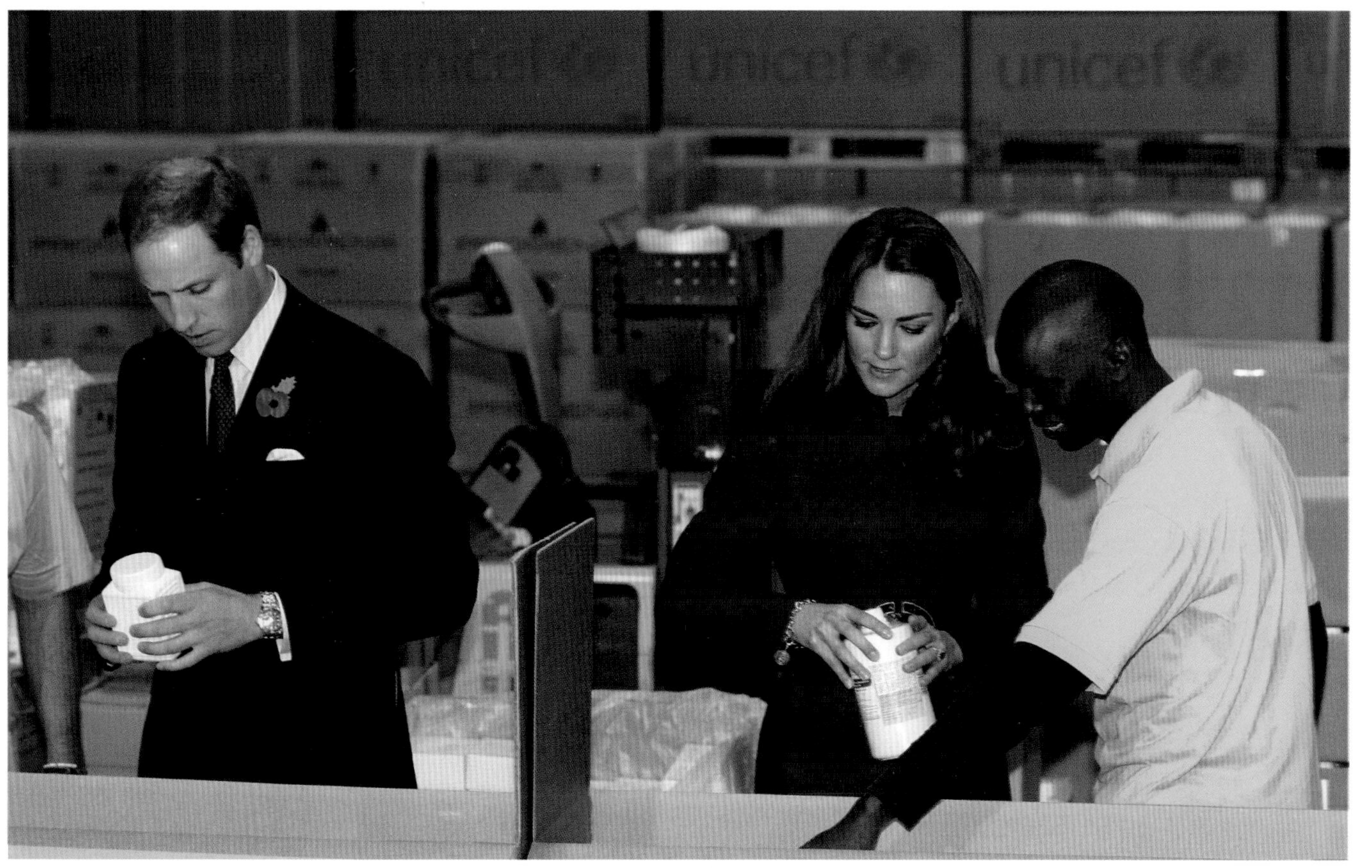

ABOVE: *Visiting the UNICEF Global Supply Centre on 2 November in Copenhagen. The huge supply centre sources supplies and packs and distributes the food, water, vaccines and emergency medical kits for children around the globe.*

couples visited a distribution centre where they helped UNICEF workers pack boxes of aid and discovered more about this humanitarian disaster.

The visit had been arranged at short notice after the Duke and Duchess became troubled by the famine in East Africa, which was said to be affecting 13 million people and putting 320,000 children in imminent risk of starvation. A spokesman for St James's Palace said: "The Duke and Duchess of Cambridge have been deeply moved over the past few weeks by the desperate plight of hundreds of thousands of seriously ill children in East Africa, a part of the world they know well and which is dear to them. Going to Copenhagen to view the supplies heading out to the famine zones was their idea as they are very troubled by the situation. The British public have already been very generous, but the royal couple wish to do what they can to help maintain global attention on the worsening situation."

Catherine told one volunteer on the production line that she and William were planning to go on a humanitarian mission to Africa in 2012. She also told journalists: "We really need to put the spotlight back on this terrible crisis."

Eleven days after the Danish visit, the Duchess attended her first Remembrance Day service in Whitehall. William followed his father and grandparents and laid a wreath at the Cenotaph. His wife appeared on a balcony of the Foreign Office with Camilla, Sophie Wessex and Princess Anne's husband, Vice-Admiral Tim Laurence. Both William's and Catherine's grandfathers served during the Second World War: Prince Philip in the Royal Navy while Catherine's grandfather, Peter Middleton, trained pilots.

ABOVE: *Camilla and Catherine are joined on the Foreign Office balcony by Sophie Wessex and Princess Anne's husband Vice-Admiral Sir Timothy Laurence to observe the Remembrance Day Ceremony at the Cenotaph in London on 13 November 2011.*

Protocol dictates that royal ladies always wear black and Catherine wore a black double-breasted coat designed by Diane Von Furstenberg with matching hat by Jane Corbett. She wore two poppies in her lapel.

Later in the month, Catherine and William joined the Queen and Prince Philip, along with Charles and Camilla, for a reception for the media held at Buckingham Palace to mark the Queen's Diamond Jubilee in the coming year. The royal party shook hands with a small line-up of journalists including Andrew Marr, Philip Schofield and Fearne Cotton before breaking off into different groups to talk to the other 350 writers and photographers.

Catherine, who was wearing a £1,400 emerald-green Mulberry shirtdress with a Peter Pan collar, was quickly surrounded by eager press representatives and joked about how nerve-wracking it was facing a room full of journalists.

A week later there was another family get-together when the Cambridges joined Charles and Camilla for a night out at the Royal Albert Hall to attend a concert given by Garry Barlow, which raised about £400,000 for The Prince's Trust and The Foundation of Prince William and Prince Harry. Before the concert began, the Take That star met the royal guests at a reception and told them: "I hope you enjoy tonight, I hope it's not too loud," to which Prince William joked: "The louder the better!"

Catherine chose high-street fashion for this event, teaming a £69.99 black-and-grey dress from Zara with a black Ralph Lauren jacket, while Camilla wore an outfit by one of her favourite designers, Anna Valentine.

Christmas is very much a family occasion for the House of Windsor. On 19 December Catherine was a guest at a lunch hosted by the Queen at Buckingham Palace for the entire royal family, including the monarch's Kent and Gloucester cousins and their children and grandchildren.

The same evening William and Catherine attended *The Sun* Military Awards

Ceremony at the Imperial War Museum in London where Catherine looked stunning in a black velvet strapless dress from Alexander McQueen Studio – they also designed her wedding dress. With this she wore a silver necklace with matching earrings and a bracelet, which she had received as a wedding present.

Two days later the couple visited Centrepoint, the charity for homeless people that Diana first introduced William to when he was still quite young. A spokesperson said: "It is one of the prince's oldest patronages and is particularly dear to his heart. He has been keen to show the Duchess the charity's work in action. It will be the first time she has visited a project of this kind in this country and she has been looking forward to it immensely."

Catherine, dressed in an olive-green Ralph Lauren jersey dress and black suede boots, took part in a "Workwise" programme which enables those attending to

BELOW: *Prince William, Duke of Cambridge and Catherine, Duchess of Cambridge attend the wreath-laying ceremony at the National War Memorial on day one of the royal couple's North American tour on 30 June 2011 in Ottawa, Canada.*

prepare themselves for applying for jobs. She also took part in a cookery class, making mince pies and gingerbread.

The couple then headed for Sandringham, the Queen's Norfolk home, where it was announced that Prince Philip had been rushed to Papworth Hospital with chest pains on 23 December. William is particularly close to his grandfather and it was a worrying time for him and all his family. Fortunately, the Duke improved after having a coronary stent fitted, although he had to miss Christmas with the Queen for the first time since 1956.

On Christmas Day William and Harry drove with their cousins Peter, Zara, Beatrice and Eugenie to visit the Duke while Catherine stayed with the Queen. Earlier in the day, the usual crowd of a thousand or so well-wishers swelled to 3,000 to see the Duchess walk to church on her first Christmas Day with the family. Wearing a deep-claret coat with a Jane Corbett hat, she looked relaxed and happy as she took flowers and cards from well-wishers after the service before walking back to the "Big House" for lunch. For Catherine it was the perfect end to the most momentous year of her life.

BELOW: *Catherine, William, Prince Charles and the Duchess of Cornwall pose for photographs with British singer-songwriter Gary Barlow ahead of a fund-raising concert at the Royal Albert Hall in London on 6 December 2011.*

OPPOSITE: *Catherine meets guests at a reception held by Queen Elizabeth II for members of the media to mark the following year's Diamond Jubilee at Buckingham Palace on 28 November 2011.*

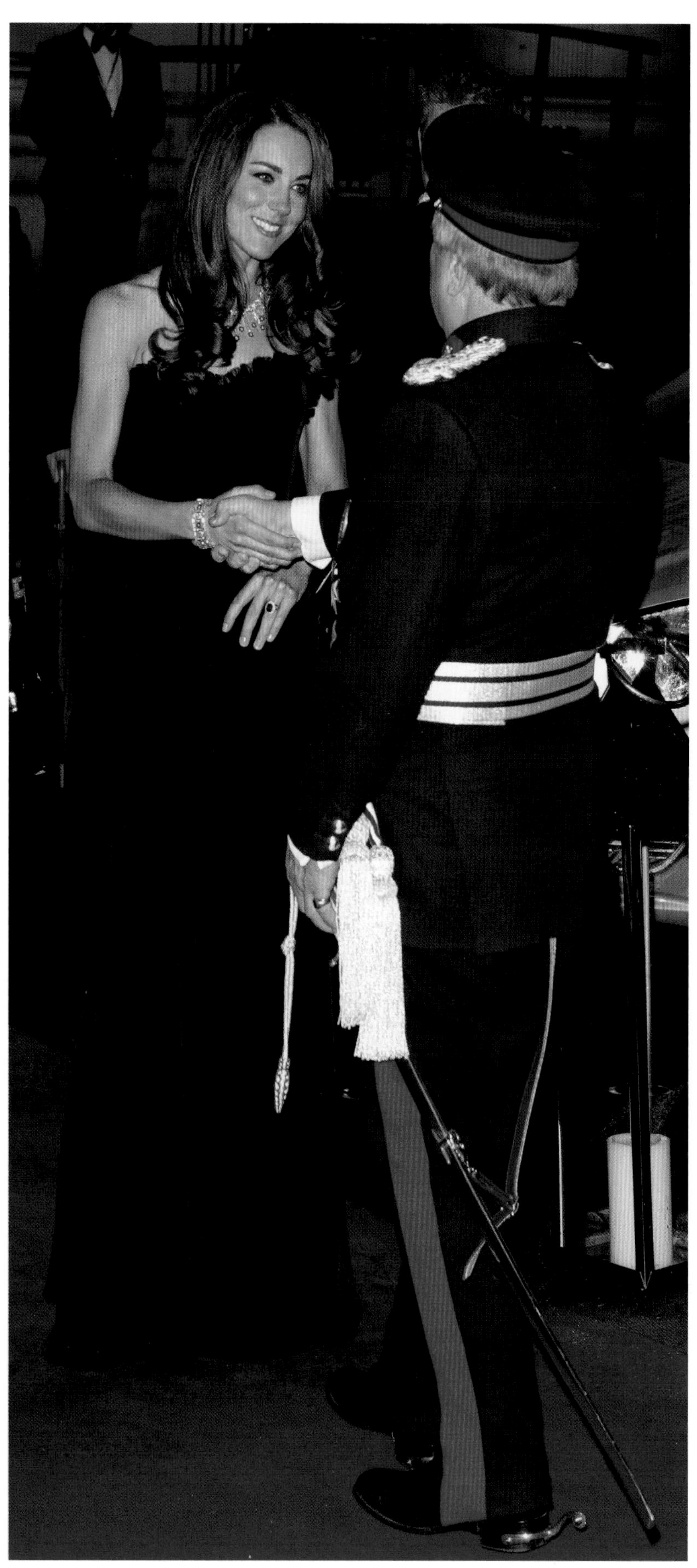

LEFT: *Catherine, Duchess of Cambridge greets Sir David Brewer, Lord-Lieutenant of Greater London, as she attends* The Sun *Military Awards at the Imperial War Museum on 19 December 2011.*

RIGHT, ABOVE: *Catherine and William at a "healthy living cookery session" during a visit to Centrepoint's Camberwell Foyer on 21 December. The national charity Centrepoint provides housing and support to improve the lives of homeless young people aged 16–25.*

RIGHT, BELOW: *The Duchess of Cambridge meets members of the public as she leaves Sandringham Church after the traditional Christmas Day service on 25 December 2011.*

TEAMWORK

The spring of 2012 would see Catherine taking on more solo royal appearances while William was deployed to the South Atlantic for six weeks. The Duchess also joined the Queen on two of her engagements in March, seeing for herself at first hand how the most experienced member of the royal family carries out her duties.

LEFT: *The Duchess waves as she arrives for an official visit to the Art Room facilities at Rose Hill Primary School in Oxford, on 21 February 2012. During her visit Catherine let slip to schoolchildren that her new puppy is called Lupo.*

After seeing in the New Year at Bucklebury with the Middletons, William and Catherine kept a low profile in January, only appearing officially in public once, when they attended the premiere of the film *War Horse*. Based on the children's novel by Michael Morpurgo, *War Horse* has enjoyed stage success in London's West End production, which both William and his grandparents, the Queen and Prince Philip, have been to see.

The premiere took place at the Odeon, Leicester Square, on 8 January, the eve of Catherine's thirtieth birthday. Looking stunning in an Alice Temperley cream dress with an outer layer of black lace patterned with leaves and flowers, the Duchess was shielded from the rain by an umbrella held by Prince William.

The film's director, Steven Spielberg, was thrilled that William and Catherine could attend. "It's a very prestigious honour", he told the media beforehand, "because they represent an entirely new era in British royalty that has the entire world excited." The following day in an interview on *BBC Breakfast*, Spielberg revealed that Catherine had at one point discreetly shed a tear. "I was sitting next to her and all I know is at one point my wife, who was sitting to my right, right in front of my face she passed a Kleenex... I saw the Kleenex go across my face, arrive and stop but I didn't want to intrude on her experience watching *War Horse* so I never glanced over," he said. "According to my peripheral vision her eyes were dabbed."

There were no tears later in the month when the couple headed for the Caribbean island of Mustique for a family break with Catherine's parents, sister Pippa and brother James. They stayed in a property called Aurora House, which lies on the east coast of the island, costs £11,500 a week to hire and offers peace, seclusion and spectacular ocean views. Mustique was made famous by the late Princess Margaret, who built a villa, Les Jolies Eaux, on a secluded part of the island given to her as a wedding present by her friend Lord Glenconner. William and Catherine have also fallen in love with it and have holidayed there at least four times in the past.

In the first week of February, William arrived in the Falkland Islands for a six-week tour of duty as an RAF search and rescue pilot. The deployment, in the run-up to the thirtieth anniversary of the Falklands War of 1982, led to criticism by some Argentineans reported in the press that it constituted an "act of provocation" and that the prince would be wearing the uniform of a "conqueror" during his time there.

Meanwhile in the UK it was announced that Catherine would be undertaking some solo engagements during William's absence. In a statement released on 4 January, Catherine's office revealed that the Duchess would become patron of four organizations: Action on Addiction, East Anglia's Children's Hospices, The Art Room and the National Portrait Gallery, London. In addition she would become a volunteer in the Scout Association,

OPPOSITE: *The Duke and Duchess attend the UK premiere of the film* War Horse *at the Odeon Leicester Square in London, on 8 January 2012.*

ABOVE: *Prince William and his crew prepare for their first sortie of a six-week deployment in the Mount Pleasant Complex on the Falkland Islands.*

LEFT: *The prince operates a Sea King Mk 3 helicopter during the search and rescue team's first sortie in the Falklands, on 4 February 2012. This was his first overseas operational deployment.*

RIGHT: *Catherine arrives at London's National Portrait Gallery to view the "Lucian Freud Portraits" exhibition on 8 February 2012.*

"volunteering time privately with groups in north Wales and elsewhere as opportunity arises". The statement concluded: "The Duchess has chosen to support organizations that complement the charitable work already undertaken by her husband."

Her first solo engagement occurred just a few days after William's departure. Catherine faced a blitz of camera flashes as she arrived at the National Portrait Gallery on the evening of 8 February to attend a preview of the "Lucian Freud Portraits" exhibition.

The following Tuesday, 14 February, she travelled to Liverpool in support of Alder Hey Children's Hospital and The Brink, an alcohol-free bar in the city centre that is run by the charity Action on Addiction. There she tried the latest drink on the menu, named the "Duchess" smoothie in her honour. "It's delicious," she told the crowds after tasting the £2.50 drink made from banana, almonds, milk, honey and cream.

It was, of course, Valentine's Day and she revealed that William had sent her a card from 12,700 kilometres (7,900 miles) away in the South Atlantic and had arranged for a bouquet of flowers to be delivered.

At Alder Hey some of the patients had made their own cards to give her. Ten-year-old Ethan Harris included a poem in his which read: "You're smiley like the sun, you're bright like a star, you're light when it's dark and I love your spark." A delighted Catherine said: "Thank you, that's lovely."

OPPOSITE: *With William away in the South Atlantic, Catherine went on several day trips, including this one to Liverpool, where she visited the Alder Hey Children's Hospital on 14 February.*

ABOVE: *Catherine tries a specially made smoothie drink called the "Duchess" during a visit to The Brink, an alcohol-free bar in Liverpool. The bar is run by one of the her charities, Action on Addiction.*

Exactly a week later, the Duchess spent the day at two Oxford schools, where – as patron of The Art Room – she joined schoolchildren who are experiencing emotional and behavioural problems. The charity uses art to increase their self-esteem and confidence. At Rose Hill Primary School, Catherine put on a denim apron with "Miss Catherine" stencilled across it as she helped five pupils paint scenes from Edward Lear's poem "The Owl and the Pussycat". Later Lisa Hancock, who manages the group, said Catherine "seemed to have as much fun as the children and seemed very relaxed and in her element, I think. She had all the right language and was very calm and gentle."

The Duchess also visited the Oxford Spires Academy, for a discussion on the value of the sessions from past and present pupils. Julie Beattie, who founded

BELOW: *With William away, Catherine kept herself occupied on Valentine's Day. Here she unveils a plaque with patient Ethan Harris during her visit to Alder Hey Children's Hospital in Liverpool, 14 February 2012.*

The Art Room, said: "We are overwhelmed to have our Royal Patron here. We are a small charity, and to have that recognition is fantastic."

After her solo engagements, Catherine carried out two engagements with the Queen, at the latter's suggestion. A few weeks earlier, a senior aide had revealed: "The Duchess is keen to learn from the Queen and readily accepted the invitation to join her."

On 1 March, three generations of royal ladies – the Queen, Camilla Duchess of Cornwall and Catherine Duchess of Cambridge – travelled in the same car to visit Fortnum & Mason's store to mark the refurbishment of Piccadilly in central London. Inside, they toured different areas of the classic shop: the Queen viewed honey and preserves, Camilla toured the bakery section and Catherine was escorted to the tea area and the confectionary display. Later the royal party met for tea with 150 people involved in the Piccadilly regeneration.

A week later, Catherine joined the Queen and Prince Philip on the first day of their nationwide Diamond Jubilee tour in celebration of the Queen's 60 years on the throne. They travelled overnight on the royal train to Leicester,

ABOVE: *Catherine chats to Doctor Lisa Howell during her tour of the wards on her visit to Alder Hey Children's Hospital.*

The
ArtRoom
Miss
Catherine

where the two royal ladies attended a student fashion show at De Montfort University, a multi-faith service at the Cathedral and a short ceremony at the Clock Tower in the city centre, where the Queen received a gift to mark her Jubilee.

For Catherine it was part of a remarkable year, during which she had been transformed from being the shy bride accompanying Prince William on his engagements to taking on her own solo duties with ease and fitting seamlessly into royal life.

LEFT: *Catherine wears a personalized "Miss Catherine" apron during a visit to The Art Room facilities at Rose Hill Primary School, Oxford on 21 February 2012. As patron of The Art Room, a charity which works with children to increase their self-confidence and self-esteem, the Duchess visited two schools in Oxford.*

ABOVE: *Very much hands-on, Catherine spent two hours painting with children at Rose Hill Primary School, Oxford in her role as patron of The Art Room, proving she wants to be more than a mere figurehead.*

RIGHT: *A taste of things to come. Catherine views a Diamond-Jubilee-themed iced cake while visiting Fortnum & Mason store in Piccadilly on 1 March 2012.*

LEFT: *Three ladies in blue. Catherine, Camilla and the Queen outside the famous store Fortnum & Mason as Her Majesty prepares to unveil a plaque to mark the regeneration of London's Piccadilly.on 1 March 2012.*

ABOVE: *Catherine joined the Queen and Prince Philip in Leicester on 8 March 2012 for the first leg of the Diamond Jubilee tour of Britain. The Queen is close to her granddaughter-in-law and regards her as a terrific asset to the monarchy.*

RIGHT: *The Queen and Catherine watch a fashion show together at De Montfort University; this was their first joint engagement of the day in Leicester on 8 March 2012.*

THE FUTURE

In this Diamond Jubilee year we are reminded that the Queen took on the burden of sovereignty at the age of just 25. William's mother Diana was even younger, aged only 20, when she married the heir to the throne, and she had very little preparation for her new role in life.

LEFT: *Catherine talks to scouts and guides outside Leicester Cathedral on 8 March 2012. The Duchess was a Brownie in her youth and has chosen to be a volunteer with the Scout Association, working privately with groups in North Wales and other areas.*

William and Catherine are fortunate. With both the Queen and Prince Charles in good health, it could be several decades before they succeed as king and queen. In the meantime they have the opportunity to allow William to concentrate on his air-force career and for Catherine to learn the ropes in an organized and relaxed way. The couple are both thoroughly enjoying the time they are able to spend together away from the gaze of the public and media in their isolated home on the picturesque island of Anglesey. The prince may well choose to extend his length of service by another two years, which would keep him busy until 2015, and would also allow the couple to raise a family away from the constant scrutiny that he and Harry experienced growing up in the 1980s and 1990s.

The couple are keen to have children. Catherine has said, "I hope we will be able to have a happy family ourselves." William has also spoken of his

BELOW: *On 2 June 1953 the newly crowned Queen Elizabeth II waves to the crowd from the balcony at Buckingham Palace. Her children Prince Charles and Princess Anne stand between her and the Queen Mother.*

ABOVE: *The Coronation coach leaves Buckingham Palace en route to Westminster Abbey in 1953.*

desire, saying: "Obviously we want a family so we'll have to start thinking about that."

A recent change in the centuries-old rules of succession could have interesting implications for any children the Cambridges might have. In October 2011, British Prime Minister David Cameron wrote to his Commonwealth counterparts to explain how he wanted to change the discriminatory law which stated that women had to take their place behind younger royal males in the line of succession. He also outlined his plan to lift the traditional ban on members of the Royal Family who marry Roman Catholics from being able to succeed to the throne.

Until now, Prince William would have had to renounce his claim to the throne had he wished to marry a member of the Roman Catholic Church and had she been unwilling to change her faith, in the way Prince Michael of Kent forfeited his place in the line of succession when he married the catholic Marie Christine von Reibnitz on 30 June 1978. Also until now, if William and Catherine's eldest child was a girl and the second was a son, male primogeniture

ABOVE: *The Prince and Princess of Wales leave St Paul's Cathedral on their wedding day on 29 July 1981. Unlike Catherine, Diana was never properly trained for her role and later complained that she had been "thrown in at the deep end".*

would have meant that the boy would succeed to the throne rather than his older sister.

The leaders of the 16 Commonwealth countries where the Queen is head of state unanimously approved the changes at a summit in Perth, Australia, during the Commonwealth Heads of Government Meeting on 28 October 2011. This means that a first-born daughter of the Duke and Duchess of Cambridge would take precedence over younger brothers, and any children born of the marriage can marry a Roman Catholic without losing their place in the succession.

At the moment, however, "family" is the two of them and their cocker spaniel, whose name – Lupo – the Duchess let slip when she was on a visit to a primary school in Oxford in February. The couple have been spotted walking Lupo on the beach near their Anglesey home and Catherine, accompanied by a detective, took him for a run in Kensington Gardens while William was away in the South Atlantic.

When they do start a family they will need more space, and they will move into Princess Margaret's former apartment, No 1a Kensington Palace, after refurbishment is completed in 2013. They may also use Harewood Park in Herefordshire as a country residence. This eco-friendly, six-bedroom mansion has being built under the direction of the Prince of Wales, who has asked for solar panels and wall insulation made from sheep's wool.

While William concentrates on his career, Catherine will take on more charity work. Rather than inheriting her patronages en masse as previous royal ladies have had to do, she is more likely to investigate each organization first to ensure she can properly contribute something to help. She definitely doesn't want to be a mere figurehead.

Diana was very insecure in her early years as a married royal while Sarah, the Duchess of York who was married to Prince Andrew from 1986–96, appeared to be quite the opposite. Catherine's dignified and more measured approach is a throwback to early generations. She has the Queen's steadfast determination and regality combined with the Queen Mother's charm and easy smile. Like them, she intends to remain a more remote figure, solidly supporting the work of Prince William, rather than trying to outshine him as a media star.

That said, she is rapidly becoming a style icon and one of the world's legendary beauties. Comparisons will always be made with Diana, and both

BELOW: *The Queen opened the 2011 Commonwealth Heads of Government Meeting (CHOGM) in Perth on 28 October. During the meeting, the prime ministers of the 16 nations for which Elizabeth is head of state voted to amend the succession laws to allow a first-born girl to succeed and to permit royals to marry Catholics without losing their place in the line of succession.*

William and Catherine are desperate to ensure that history doesn't repeat itself. They are on record as saying they've learned lessons from the past. Their future will be built on a sounder base than his mother's was, and this should enable them to take the monarchy into the second half of the twenty-first century with a deft hand, combining the best of the past with their own style, flair and individuality.

OPPOSITE: *The Queen delivers a speech during a banquet at the Pan Pacific Perth Hotel as part of the Commonwealth Heads of Government Meeting on 28 October 2011 in Perth, Australia.*

BELOW: *Kensington Palace was William's childhood home. He and Catherine will take up residence here in 2013 following the refurbishment of Princess Margaret's apartment.*

LEFT: *As part of the build up to the 2012 London Olympics, on 15 March Catherine tours the Riverside Arena in the Olympic Park and meets the men's and women's hockey teams for Great Britain. Catherine even manages to find time to join in a hockey game.*

ABOVE: *Catherine poses with the Irish Guards at Aldershot Barracks on St Patrick's Day, 17 March.*

RIGHT: *Catherine shows how far she has come during her first year as Her Royal Highness The Duchess of Cambridge, when she gives her first public speech at the Treehouse Children's Centre in Ipswich on 19 March 2012.*

The publishers would like to thank Getty Images and their photographers/agents for their kind permission to reproduce the pictures in this book.

3-4. Phil Noble/WPA Pool, 8-9. Hugo Burnand/AFP, 10. Andrew Milligan/WPA Pool, 11. Ian West/WPA Pool, 12. Jeff J. Mitchell, 13. Indigo, 14. & 15. John Stillwell/WPA Pool, 16. Carl Court/AFP (top), 16. Lewis Whyld/WPA Pool (bottom), 17. Stillwell/WPA Pool, 18-19. Chris Jackson, 20. Andrew Yates/AFP, 21. MoD Crown Copyright, 22. Indigo, 23. Andrew Yates/AFP (top), 23. Hulton Archive (bottom), 24. Bob Thomas/ Popperfoto, 25. Travel Ink, 26-27. Mark Large/Pool, 28. Steve Parsons/WPA Pool, 29. & 30. Timothy A. Clary/AFP, 31. Samir Hussein/WireImage, 32. David Rose/Pool, 33. Samir Hussein/WireImage, 34. Mark Large/Pool, 35. Arthur Edwards/Pool, 36. Chris Jackson (top), 36. Arthur Edwards/Pool (bottom), 37. Samir Hussein/WireImage, 38. Chris Jackson (top), 38. Samir Hussein/WireImage (bottom), 39. Samir Hussein/ WireImage, 40. Chris Jackson (top), Samir Hussein/WireImage (bottom), 41. Chris Jackson 42-43. Steve Granitz/WireImage, 44. Toby Melville/AFP, 45. Chris Jackson/WPA Pool, 46. Kevork Djansezian, 47. Frazer Harrison, 48. Lionel Hahn/WPA Pool, 49. & 50. Frazer Harrison, 51. Chris Jackson, 52. Ian Volger/Pool, 53. Terry Fincher/Princess Diana Archive, 54. Chris Jackson, 55. Mark Large/Pool, 56. John Stillwell/Pool (top), Valerie Macon/AFP (bottom), 57. John Shearer/WireImage, 58-59. Chris Jackson, 60. Indigo, 61. Arthur Edwards/AFP, 62. Anwar Hussein/WireImage, 63. & 64. Dan Kitwood, 65. Oli Scarff, 66. Chris Jackson/ WPA Pool, 67. Steve Parsons/AFP, 68. Chris Jackson, 69. Carl Court/AFP, 70-71. Dave M. Benett, 72. & 73. Indigo, 74, 75. & 76. Carl Court/AFP, 77. Clive Mason (top), 77. Leon Neal (bottom), 78. WireImage, 79, 80 & 81. Dylan Martinez/AFP, 82-83. Indigo, 84. Gerry Penny/AFP, 85. Tony Woolliscroft/WireImage, 86. David Jones/AFP, 87. Steve Parsons/WPA Pool, 88. Terry Fincher/Princess Diana Archive, 89. & 90. Kirsty Wigglesworth/WPA Pool, 91. Paul Burns/Clarence House, 92. Lefteris Pitarakis/WPA Pool, 93. Lefteris Pitarakis/AFP, 94-95. Chris Jackson, 96. Samir Hussein/WireImage, 97. Jeff J. Mitchell, 98. Indigo, 99. Samir Hussein/WireImage, 100. Ben Stansall/AFP, 101. Gareth Fuller/WPA Pool, 102. Indigo, 103. Ben Stansall/ WPA Pool (top), 103. Chris Jackson (bottom), 105-106. Steve Parsons/AFP, 106. Jon Furniss/WireImage, 108. Sgt Andy Malthouse/MoD, 109. Indigo, 110. Phil Noble/AFP, 111. Mark Large/AFP, 112. Phil Noble/ AFP, 113. Paul Edwards/WPA Pool, 114. Steve Parsons/WPA Pool, 115. Steve Parsons/WPA Pool (top), 115. Leon Neal/WPA Pool, 116. Ferdaus Shamim/WireImage, 117. Anwar Hussein/WireImage (top), Oli Scarff/ WPA Pool (bottom), 118-119. Matt Cardy, 120. & 121. Hulton Archive, 122. Jayne Fincher/Princess Diana Archive, 123. Paul Kane/AFP, 124. Ron D'Raine/Pool, 125. Tim Graham, 126. Chris Jackson/WPA Pool, 126. Chris Jackson (top), Kirsty Wigglesworth/WPA Pool (bottom)

Every effort has been made to acknowledge correctly and contact the source and/or copyright holder of each picture and Carlton Books Limited apologises for any unintentional errors or omissions, which will be corrected in future editions of this book.

Thanks to Hayley Newman for her assistance on this book.

Publishing Credits

Editorial Manager: Vanessa Daubney
Executive Editor: Jennifer Barr
Copyeditor: Jane Birch
Additional editorial work: Catherine Rubinstein
Art Editor: Katie Baxendale
Design: Lorna Morris
Picture Research Manager: Steve Behan
Production Manager: Maria Petalidou